Dinka Agaar Warrior
by Isaac Tieng

A GLIMPSE OF AFRICA

I've always had an adventurous spirit, and that spirit has led me throughout the years to many exotic countries with cultures different from my own. It has carried me to the distant shores of my childhood dreams, to places like Hong Kong, Taiwan, Singapore, and others. And while I have been blessed to visit so many foreign lands, there is still one that remains unseen. It calls to me in a strong and compelling voice and remains my greatest dream of all: the wilds of Africa.

My friends who have visited the faraway continent and returned with photos and fascinating stories of their adventures have only fueled my passion to behold its beauty. I've listened in awe to their tales of close encounters with ferocious lions, and have felt the very grip of their fears when spending sleepless nights while listening to the sounds and snorts of wild animals circling round their tents. I've viewed countless numbers of breathtaking photos of African wildlife roaming freely in their natural habitats, often envisioning myself as the photographer of such photos, having shot them while traveling over uncharted terrain on the vast plains of my imagination.

When traveling on such imaginary journeys, I have visited remote villages inhabited by African natives who chant in unknown tongues while dancing to the beat of tribal drums that sound throughout the night in thunderous rhythm. Their ebony bodies, silhouettes against the rising flames of fire about which they circle in continuous patterns of jumps and frenzied movements. My visions stop short, however, when contemplating if these natives are a friendly people, or vicious warriors like those depicted on early Tarzan episodes, their faces shrouded behind a veil of mystery in the hollowed heads of once fierce leopards. I can only imagine the final scene, as I have never had such real-life encounters with natives from Africa, having long ago resigned myself to stolen glimpses of their mirrored reflections on the pages of *National Geographic* or

4

the evening news. The most memorable of those images are not those of fierce tribal warriors, but rather those of African refugees living in Ethiopian squatter camps in the late 1980s.

I remember watching the evening news one night when a multitude of the African men, women, and children filled the screen. Having fled their countries due to civil war and drought, the refugees had traveled by foot for months before reaching the distant borders of Ethiopia. I looked in horror at their frail bodies, ravaged by starvation and disease, and their images were forever etched into the walls of my heart and mind. Many of the refugees, especially the young children, had deteriorated to the point where they could no longer walk or stand; with quiet resign, they waited for their certain deaths with welcomed reprieve. I wanted desperately to do something, anything I could to help them, but Africa seemed so far away. What could I possibly do? Ultimately, I did the only thing I could do and simply said a prayer on their behalf, and then with the rest of the world, I turned the channel hoping someone else would come to their rescue.

In the years that followed, their images continued to haunt me, but I heard very little more about them. I'm not sure if that's why I incorrectly assumed that someone had, in fact, come to their aid, or if I, after marrying and having children of my own, simply became caught up in the worries and cares of my own life. But as time passed, their images slowly began to fade and with them my lifelong dreams of visiting Africa. That is until the summer of 2001, when my life took a sudden and unexpected turn that would forever change the course of my future.

I finally got my long awaited glimpse of Africa that year, but the view was much different than I ever imagined, and the journey unlike any other before it. For it was not a journey measured in miles, or one traveled across distant continents. There were no visits to rural native villages and no photographic safaris across the vast Serengeti plains. In fact, I did not travel to Africa at all, because this was a journey of my heart, one in which Africa came to me.

Prior to that summer, I had never even heard of the Lost Boys of Sudan and had no knowledge of their incredible story. And unbeknownst to me, approximately 3,800 of the young refugees had come to America that year in a resettlement program established by the United States government and the UNHCR (United Nations High Committee for Refugees). Of that first group, 85 resettled in my hometown of Jacksonville, Florida, and many were attending weekly services at my church. I couldn't help but notice them as they gathered outside the church entrance, as they were extremely hard to miss. Most were tall in stature and noticeably thin, and their skin was the darkest shade of black imaginable, making it difficult to distinguish their features from a distance. However, on those rare occasions when I did venture closer, hoping to steal a better glimpse of them, I noticed not only their strikingly handsome features, but also the scars and strange markings that were visibly etched upon their faces and bodies. The sight of them intrigued me and I became extremely curious as to who they were, but my fear of the unknown prevented me from asking them and I simply continued to observe them safely from a distance.

Initially, I assumed them to be from Haiti, as so many from that country have taken refuge in our coastal state. But these young men looked different than any other refugees I had ever seen, and yet somehow they seemed familiar. Several weeks later, my good friend and fellow church member, Lynn Lamoureux, finally satisfied my curiosity and told me of their story.

She explained that they had come originally from Sudan, Africa, and that due to civil war and famine, they had been forced to flee their homeland at early ages. Most had become separated from their parents and families in the process and were now assumed to be orphans. Foreign aid workers, comparing them to the fictional characters of the movie Peter Pan, had named them "The Lost Boys of Sudan." But as I soon learned, their lives had been anything but a fairytale.

In one single raid by the government of Sudan's "Arab Muslim Militia," thousands of innocent men, women, and children from the South of Sudan were slaughtered and multiple generations erased. Countless others were captured and sold into slavery or left to wander alone in the desolate wilds of Africa, with no food, water, or shelter. The young men who gathered outside our church were some of the more fortunate ones who had survived this holocaust, in part, by traveling some thousand miles on foot to refugee camps located in Ethiopia and Kenya. In the nine plus years of living in such camps, they suffered unspeakable hardships, surviving on rations less than that of the average American cat. But in spite of their hardships, they consider themselves lucky because they, unlike so many others, had survived.

Although their new life in America would afford them the freedom of which they had long been deprived, it also provided a host of other opportunities as well. The Lost Boys soon obtained jobs, enabling them to live independently for the first time in their lives. And more importantly, many continued their education, securing not only their futures in America, but also in Sudan, should they one day choose to return. America was truly a land of golden opportunities for them, and their new lives were those beyond their wildest dreams.

For the first time, they were enjoying such luxuries as electricity, air conditioning, running water, and flushing toilets. It didn't matter that they were living in low-income apartments, because in light of such luxuries, they felt as if they were living like kings. Those living in Jacksonville received the additional bonus of living on the coast, and upon seeing the ocean for the first time, they marveled at the magnitude and beauty of it. "If you swim beyond the waves, to the other side," they asked, "what city will you reach?" They were also curious to know if they could find gold and diamonds on the beach, in addition to the beautiful shells that lay scattered across the sand. Some were even more anxious to know if crocodiles lurked beneath the water's surface.

Those living in the colder climates of the U.S. experienced an even greater phenomenon: snow. And although it was a fascinating sight for them to behold, it was also one in which they quickly agreed they could live without. "It is very cold! I do not like it!" they complained. I once asked one of them if he had ever seen a snowman, but my question went unanswered. I then asked him if he even knew what a snowman was and he replied, "Yes, it is a man who works in the snow!"

America was filled with many strange and exciting wonders for these young men who had walked from the most remote villages of Africa, crashing head on into the twenty-first century. To them, this was paradise.

When meeting the Lost Boys for the first time, Venda Buchac, of Lutheran Social Services (the sponsoring agency for the Jacksonville Lost Boys), compared them to Mowgli, the fictional character in Rudyard Kiplings' *The Jungle Book*. She would not be the last to make such comparisons, or the last to be taken in by their childlike innocence and charming personalities. These young men and their incredible stories touched people from all walks of life, from movie stars and politicians, to the average housewife. And I was no exception. When hearing their story for the first time, my eyes filled with tears and I felt a deep stirring in my soul. I knew that helping them was not an option. It was a call to my heart from God and I responded. I felt compelled to be a mother to these young men who couldn't even remember the faces of their own mothers. So in the past three years, that is what I have become to many of these wonderful and courageous young men who now call me "Mom" or "Mama Joan."

I don't believe it is a coincidence that the Lost Boys came into my life or I theirs, as my family and I had been waiting to adopt another child for many years. My young son had been pleading for an older brother and would not be dissuaded, even when we were advised to adopt a much younger child. In finding the Lost Boys, whom my son lovingly calls his "African brothers," God has answered all of our prayers, many times over.

However, not all our friends and family shared in our enthusiasm to help them. Initially, some of our loved ones thought I had lost my mind for becoming involved with those "natives from Africa," and they frequently voiced their objections in a bombardment of questions and concerns. "How do you know those guys don't have AIDS or some other sort of contagious diseases? What if you catch something from them? Aren't you scared to be alone with them? How do you know they won't try to hurt you?"

Initially, some of those same questions crossed my own mind, and if I'm to be perfectly honest, I must say there were times in the beginning of our relationship when I was somewhat frightened by them. Not because of the different color of skin or because they had done anything to alarm me, but rather because of the extreme differences in our cultures.

I remember the first time I visited one of their apartments alone at night. I knocked on their door and my heart pounded with fear at the sound of loud voices permeating through the door. It was obvious that a large crowd was gathered inside, and it suddenly dawned on me that I might be intruding. I had been unable to call them in advance because they had no telephone, and now, as I stood on their dimly lit porch, my only thought was to turn and run. I had already knocked on the door, however, and my only escape was that of the long and brightly lit stairwell below me. *Surely they would catch me in the act if I attempt to flee!* I reasoned. *But then again, maybe they wouldn't recognize me from behind.* Throwing all cautions aside, I turned, ready to run like the wind, when the door slowly began to open. Looking back, I realize that they were probably just as frightened of me as I was of them, because as I walked into the room and a faint ray of light swept across the darkened apartment, their once loud voices fell completely silent. The boys had been accustomed to socializing in the dark while living in Africa because they had no electricity. But for me, it was a little unsettling as I walked into the dark room and was greeted by a sea of large white eyes that stared curiously at me, anticipating my every move. Had I not been so nervous, I might have laughed at the humor of it, because it was extremely reminiscent of scenes from cartoon shows where the characters find themselves in deep, dark caves or railway tunnels and the only thing visible are mysterious blinking eyes scattered across the screen. But in my mind, my only thoughts were *Oh my God! What am I doing here? I really must be crazy!*

Having admitted to those earlier fears, however, I must tell you that they were completely unfounded, as the Lost Boys are some of the kindest and most trustworthy young men I have ever met. I must also acknowledge that there is something incredibly powerful about being at a place in your life where you know you are fulfilling your predetermined purpose. I knew without a shadow of a doubt that helping these boys was something I was meant to do, and the knowledge of that realization brought with it an inner peace and determination to do the things that I normally could not. In a very short period of time, I became consumed by an overwhelming love for these young men, which enabled me to look beyond our cultural differences and the different colors of our skin and love them beyond human reasoning—the way a mother loves her children. And although my Christian faith instructs me not to worry, I found it increasingly difficult not to. In fact, I often joked with the guys, asking "What's the number one job of mothers in America?" They would reply, "It is to worry about their children." And worry I did, frequently waking in the middle of the night worrying about one thing or another.

When one of the boys named Valentino went into the hospital for a liver biopsy, I stayed by his bedside from 7 a.m. to 7 p.m. for fear that the doctors and nurses would not understand his questions, or better yet that he wouldn't understand their answers. Valentino was extremely shy to begin with and his English was minimal. Therefore, when Americans spoke in slang, he, as well as the other boys, was completely baffled. One of the nurses asked him to "scooch" down on the bed and he looked at her like she was speaking Alien. He had no idea what "scooch" meant. Trying to explain to him that she needed to draw blood from his veins was even more challenging. I remember watching as the nurses repeatedly stuck his arms with needles, and I was amazed by the fact that he never flinched, not even once. It occurred to me that, perhaps after enduring so much pain and suffering in his life, Valentino had somehow taught himself to block it. I said a silent prayer at the thought, asking God to prevent him from ever having to endure such pain and suffering again.

Thankfully, his biopsy was a success, and like most procedures performed in American hospitals, he was quickly released and sent home. Of course, I continued to worry about him throughout the night, wearing holes in my carpet while pacing back and forth counting the hours until I could call and check on him. He had been told to monitor his temperature for the next several days, but he had never even seen a thermometer, much less used one. *What if he runs a high temperature without realizing it?* I worried. *What if he and his roommates don't know what to do and he slips into a coma, or has a seizure or something?* I knew that this was unlikely, but what can I say? I felt it my duty to worry and I've never been one to shirk responsibility. When I finally did reach him the next day, however, I found that he was much less concerned than I was. In fact he had been out playing soccer with his friends, despite warnings from the doctor that it may cause fatal bleeding. But then again, the boys were accustomed to sickness while living in Africa—they had been surrounded by it.

After coming to America, however, they assumed such sickness and disease had been left behind. They naively believed that American doctors could cure all illnesses, and that no one ever died in here. But those beliefs were soon dispelled when two of them living in our city died from incurable illnesses. The boys quickly changed their way of thinking saying that "People who go into the hospitals in America never come out."

Concerns over their health were only one of the many worrisome issues we faced following their arrival in the U.S. The issue of eating—or should I say not eating—was by far the most challenging. Many of the boys became sick following attempts at digesting our rich American foods, with some of them giving up trying altogether. Purchasing food was yet another dilemma, because the choices were so overwhelming. The boys had no idea what types of food to buy, and they had even less knowledge about how to prepare it. Storing food was yet another problem, because the boys had never used refrigerators and had no idea which foods needed to be refrigerated. Therefore, many of the perishable items were stored in pantries and cabinets, becoming spoiled. This didn't seem to bother them, however, as they sometimes ate the foods regardless, most likely considering the furry molds which covered them to be normal in a country with so many strange looking foods. I guess in some cases the spoiled foods actually tasted better than what they had been given while living in the camps. And of course, it also gave me one more reason to worry. Can anyone spell p-t-o-m-a-i-n-e poisoning?

My Sunday school class agreed to adopt one of the groups of boys, and we began delivering home-cooked meals on a weekly basis for the first few months following their arrival. I also made attempts to teach the boys how to prepare simple and nutritious meals by holding mini cooking classes in their apartment. All of the boys living in that particular complex were invited in an effort to encourage more of them to eat. But not only does it not cross their minds to eat, it also made some of them feel guilty for eating while their loved ones continue to starve in Africa. Others complain that it is a woman's job and requires too much time. Regardless of their reasons, I was often concerned about this problem, calling them almost on a daily basis to make sure that they had eaten. "Did you eat today?" I asked. "Yes we did," they replied. "What did you eat?" I would inquire further. "A piece of bread." The answer was almost always the same. A piece of bread was their usual meal for the day, after working two full-time jobs.

Hoping to further spark their interest in eating, I tried to find out which foods they enjoyed most. Initially, fried chicken was a unanimous winner, followed closely by bean and beef dishes with rice. Last, but certainly not least, was an American favorite: pizza. But even more exciting than the discovery of the foods themselves was the discovery of fast food restaurants like McDonald's, Kentucky Fried Chicken, and Domino's Pizza, where the boys could purchase their favorite foods without actually having to cook them.

Paradise? You betcha!

One of the boys told me his favorite food was pita bread. "Really?" I quizzed. "Where did you find pita bread?" He replied, "We got it from that guy, in that place." (The boys often refer to people by saying "that girl" or "that guy," even when they know their given names.) I guess I looked confused because he continued by saying "You know, Domino's!" Okay, now I got it! You mean pizza!

Another boy told me his favorite food was "whatever food was placed on his plate for that day." The mother in me smiled, and I said, "Good answer!" But the most memorable response was that of Simon Deng, who said, "Now that we are living in America, we no longer hunger for food. We hunger only for a solution for our people who remain in Southern Sudan."

I often wondered about the people they had left behind. What had become of them? I began to wonder about many things regarding the Lost Boys, but communication was often difficult in those early days due to their broken English and British accents. Another complicating factor was the rapid speed with which they spoke. I decided early on that if I was ever going to communicate with these guys, I must first learn their language. I began surfing on the Internet, searching for a means to achieve this goal, and sure enough I found an audiocassette course on Swahili. I began studying Swahili diligently for the next several months until I felt confident in my ability to speak it. I then visited their apartment, eager to show off my new skills in their native tongue.

Approaching their apartment, I heard loud voices once again and I knew that a large group of boys was gathered inside. *All the better*, I thought. *Won't they be so impressed with me?* Upon entering the apartment, I greeted each one of them with a loud "Jumbo"(hello), to which they stared back at me curiously before answering with a "hello" in English. I was not deterred by their lack of participation in my endeavor to speak their native tongue, and I proceeded to pull items from the bag of groceries I had brought with me, proudly identifying each of the items in Swahili. "Look," I said, holding up a bunch of bananas, "dizzy." *Yep, I was talking like the natives and feeling pretty impressed with myself for doing so.* The boys began speaking excitedly in their native tongue, but much too quickly for me to understand. So I simply continued to babble on in my new "second language," until one of them finally stopped me, saying, "Mama Joan, can I please ask you a question?" I said, "Sure," thinking he must want me to translate something for him. "What are you saying?" he asked. "What do you mean?" I said. "We don't understand what you are trying to say. What language are you speaking?" "Well, I'm speaking Swahili, of course. Aren't I doing it right? Is it my accent or something? Tell me how to speak it correctly." He said assuredly, "Mom, it is not your accent. We do not speak Swahili. We speak Arabic and Dinka." I said, "What?! You're from Africa. Everyone in Africa speaks Swahili!" He laughed, "No, we do not speak Swahili, and we do not know what you are talking about." I couldn't believe my ears! They didn't speak Swahili? How was that possible? And what in the world was Dinka anyway? I had never heard of such a thing! Before leaving their apartment, my ego sufficiently bruised and my tail between my legs, I firmly suggested that each of them get busy on perfecting their English because there was no way I was going to learn Arabic too!

In the months and years that have followed, I have learned many new and fascinating things about these young men. I have also realized that the more I learn about them, the more I want to know. What has become of their families for instance? Their mothers, fathers, brothers, and sisters, are they still alive? And why did the government of Sudan commit such horrible atrocities against its own people in the first place? Where was the rest of the world? Why hadn't NATO or the United States done something about it? Why had they turned their heads as if nothing was happening?

I also wondered what the boys' lives had been like prior to the civil war. What had it been like living in their African villages as small children? What did they do each day to pass the time? And where had those strange scars and markings come from? Were they the result of some tribal ritual, or had they been tortured at some point? And what was up with their teeth? Why were so many of them missing the middle portions of their lower teeth? I had so many unanswered questions, and I knew that I must somehow find the answers. And the quest for those answers has led me on an incredible journey of my own, lasting two-and-a-half years and continuing still.

During this time, I have conducted numerous interviews with the Lost Boys, compiling a chronological journal of their lives, beginning with their early childhood in Sudan and ending in the United States, where those featured in this book now reside. For the purpose of this book, I have separated those stories into individual chapters according to the period of time in which they take place. This may seem a bit unconventional to some, as most books typically follow the story of only one person, from beginning to end. But in spite of frequent claims by the boys that their stories are all the same, I beg to differ. I found that each boy holds a special story within his heart, belonging only to him, and that each story is remarkable and worthy of being told. Therefore, I have chosen this particular format in an effort to share as many of their stories with you as possible. After reading the book in its entirety, I hope that you will agree with my decision.

Also, in an effort to recover the many missing pieces of this fascinating puzzle that make up the story of the Lost Boys of Sudan, I have embarked on an extensive study into the history of Sudan and the inner workings of its government. I have condensed this information into brief synopses located at the beginning of each chapter, according to that period of time. I realize that this is also considered an unconventional method, but I have always worked outside the lines and have selected this format for several reasons. First of all, it enables the reader to establish a clear time line of the historical events leading up to the civil war, and those following, which have contributed not only to the longevity of this war, but also to the actual journey of the Lost Boys. The chosen format also enables any readers, wishing to bypass the historical synopses, to read only the stories of the boys while still achieving a reasonable understanding of their journey.

However, I feel that in order to fully appreciate the plight of the Lost Boys, and the many obstacles they have faced since coming to America, we must first travel back in time to the country of their birth, to the days prior to the civil war. It is here, in Sudan, that we can obtain a better understanding of what the boys' lives were like prior to fleeing their homeland. In doing so, perhaps we can better appreciate just how far they have come. In the next chapter, we embark on a behind-the-scenes tour into two of the Lost Boys' lives, when they lived as small children with their family and friends in their rural villages of Southern Sudan. I found them to be incredibly fascinating and hope you will feel the same.

And although a famous reporter did not write this book, or a Pulitzer Prize-winning author, of which I am neither, I can assure you of one thing: It has been written from the depths of my heart. Each of the pages is filled with love and admiration for these young men whom I proudly call my sons. Their stories are like no other I have ever heard, and it is my greatest hope that I have given them the respect and recognition they deserve.

And now please join me, as we travel back in time to the days which led up to "The Journey of the Lost Boys."

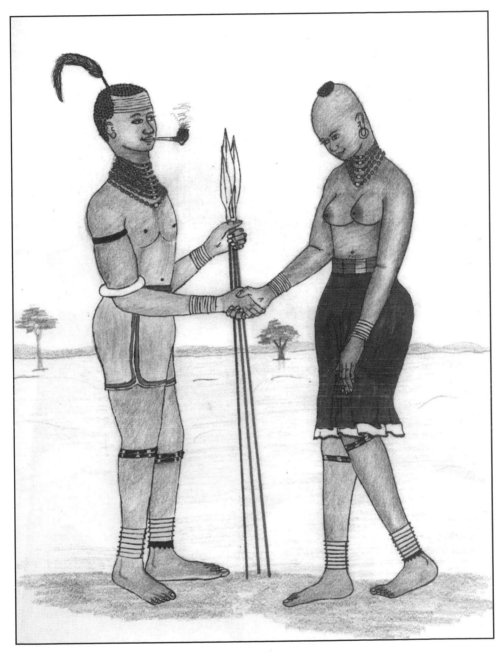

Dinka Courting Ritual
by Isaac Tieng

15

SUDAN:
THE BEGINNING

The year is 1955, and the British are in the final stages of their rule over the largest country in Africa: Sudan. With independence set for that country in the coming year, the British are faced with the difficult task of naming their successors. They must choose the future leaders of Sudan from amongst its population, who are as diverse and divided as the country itself. There are reportedly 600 different ethnic groups living in Sudan, speaking over 100 different languages. The three most prominent are the Muslims, the black Christians, and the black Animists (those who practice tribal traditions and beliefs). These groups are separated not only by their cultural, racial, and religious beliefs, but also by the different regions in which they live.

To the north, in the dry arid regions of Sudan, reside the predominantly Arab Muslim population, who for the most part are an educated people, with a small percentage earning the title of "elitists." Further to the south, in the tropical regions of Sudan, are the black Christians and Animists, who generally reside in rural villages, secluded from the outside world and modern society. They are a simple people, depending on the fertile lands that surround them for farming and the grazing of their coveted cattle, which provide not only milk and occasional meat, but also the necessary means for dowries, critical for obtaining their future wives.

One commonality shared between both North and South is the beautiful Nile River and its many tributaries that flow from it throughout the Sudan, serving as a source of life to the abundance of wildlife, cattle, and people who live there.

When all was said and done, the British named the future leaders of Sudan: the Arab Muslims of the North, who had arisen victorious over the black Christian Animists of the South. The British felt confident in their choice, assuming the educated Northerners to be better suited for the task. It was most likely a decision that would forever change the history of Sudan for the future generations that would live there.

Under British rule, the South had almost assumed autonomy to some extent, forming the beginnings of its own government. But that soon changed under the dictatorship of the Arab Muslims, who sought to unite Sudan under Islamic rule, attempting without much success to force the black Southerners to turn from their Christian and Animist beliefs and conform instead to the ways of Islam. The Southerners rose up against the Northerners, forming their own rebel militia known as "Anya-Nya," choosing to fight for their rights to practice their own religious beliefs.

The civil war that followed lasted for approximately seventeen years, throughout which time numerous leaders from both sides searched diligently for peaceful resolutions. Each fell short, however, when it came to religious dominion by the North. That is until 1972, when then ruler Jafaar Nimeiri successfully brought both sides together for the signing of the Addis Ababa Peace Treaty. This treaty granted the South, partial rights to govern itself, as well as the freedom to practice the religion of their choosing. And in the eleven years that followed its signing, Sudan knew peace once again.

Initially, Nimeiri received support from the Soviet Union, but later broke ties with the communists following several failed attempts on their part to overthrow him. He shifted his alliance instead toward an extremist Islamic group known as the National Islamic Front (NIF), who strongly opposed the Addis Ababa Treaty, arguing that it gave the South too many religious freedoms and placed Christianity in an equal position with Islam. The NIF pressured Nimeiri to establish a new Islamic government whereby "unbelievers" could not be placed in positions over "Muslim believers." The proposed political structure would essentially prevent the black Christians/Animists of the South from holding any of the higher positions in the Sudanese government. The NIF also pressured Nimeiri to enforce *Sharia*, or Islamic Law, in Sudan to which he initially resisted. They responded to his reluctance with three armed attempts to overthrow him, twice with the help of Libya. Their efforts proved unsuccessful, however, and the Addis Ababa Treaty remained in place. But religious tensions continued to mount between North and South, resulting in a constant tug of war between the two.

In addition to that struggle came a new tension in 1978 when an American oil company, Chevron, struck oil near the town of Bentiu, an area that lay just south of the North-South border of Sudan. But the discovery of crude oil would fuel much more than the modern inventions of the West. It would soon become a source of fuel for the raging fires of mistrust that burned between the North and South of Sudan.

According to the terms of the Addis Ababa Treaty, the South was to receive any revenues generated from minerals or other deposits found on their land, including the newly discovered uranium also found on Southern soil. But in spite of the agreed upon terms established in the treaty, Chevron continued to deal secretly with Nimeiri, who had no intentions of forfeiting the lucrative revenues generated from these discoveries in the South. In 1980, he went as far as trying to redefine the boundaries separating the North and South, placing the desired land, rich in oil and uranium, in a newly defined Northern province called Unity. But Nimeiri's ploy only served to deepen the lines drawn between the North and South, and the final outcome resulted in anything but unity between the two. The South responded with outcries that escalated into riots, and Nimeiri quickly backed down at the public opposition. But the wheels of distrust had already been set into motion for the angry Southerners, and they continued to move forward at high speed.

Meanwhile, in the area of the disputed oil fields, a local group of tribesmen called the Nuer, became angry over the developments in their region and, with weapons supplied by Libya, formed a new version of the earlier Anya-Nya militia, calling it Anya-Nya II. The new rebel militia quickly became regarded as a force to be reckoned with, not only by the government troops of the North, but also by opposing rebel factions living in the South.

In the midst of rebel uprisings in the South, it appeared that trouble was also brewing among the ranks of the government of Sudan (GOS). A pay dispute developed amongst a group of Southern government soldiers from the 105th battalion stationed in the Bor region of Sudan. The dispute ended with the mutiny of soldiers from that battalion, and Khartoum (the capital of Sudan and GOS headquarters) responded by calling on Col. John Garang and the 104th battalion to intercede.

John Garang was not your typical GOS officer, as he was a Dinka tribesman from the South and a former soldier in the original Anya-Nya rebel militia. Following the signing of the Addis Ababa Treaty, he and other rebel soldiers had been incorporated into GOS forces. But unlike other rebels, Garang was highly educated, having earned his Ph.D. in agricultural economics at Iowa State University in the U.S. GOS officials felt confident in their selection of Garang for the task, knowing that if anyone could resolve the matter at hand, it was Col. John Garang.

But an unprecedented turn of events took place following his arrival to Bor. Garang made a daring and extremely bold decision that was sure to record his name in history and forever change the course of his life and military career. You see, during his many years of service in the GOS military, Garang had been privy to the inner workings of the Nimeiri regime. He had witnessed firsthand Nimeiri's abuse and blatant disregard for the rules and guidelines established under the Addis Ababa Treaty. He had also watched helplessly from the sidelines as the peace agreement between North and South disintegrated into nothing more than meaningless words. It was for these reasons, and others, that Col. Garang jumped ship and joined forces with the mutinous soldiers of the 105th battalion.

Together, the rebel soldiers fled to neighboring Ethiopia where they were welcomed with open arms by then Ethiopian ruler Mengistu Haile Mariam. The Sudanese Peoples Liberation Movement/Army (SPLM/A or SPLA) was formed and Garang ultimately emerged as leader and commander in chief. He urged the Sudanese people to rise up and rally behind the SPLM/A to "establish the united socialist Sudan, not a separate Sudan."

The majority of Anya-Nya II soldiers joined forces with the SPLM/A, but a small faction joined GOS forces, assisting the government in its fight against the SPLA. In future years, others from the South would also make such alliances with the GOS. But these alliances would pit one Southern tribe against another and only serve to weaken and prolong the South's fight for freedom.

In 1983, soon after the defection of Garang and the SPLM/A, Nimeiri pledged his full allegiance to the NIF, imposing Sharia law in Sudan. Islamic law, later known as the "September Laws," was put into effect. These laws called for extremely harsh punishments such as flogging, stoning, crucifixion, public amputation, and decapitation, and were met with opposition not only from those in the South but from many in the North as well.

Cries for peace were lost in the explosion of gunfire signaling an end to the eleven-year reprieve from civil war. Once again, the lines were drawn between North and South, and civil war returned to Sudan. But with the discovery of oil and other minerals in the South, the new civil war, which in reality was a continuation of the previous one in 1955, was redefined from one of race and religious dominion to one of greed as well. It is a war that may indeed go down in history as one of the longest and most devastating civil wars ever to be recorded, continuing for almost two decades and causing the displacement of millions of people from the South of Sudan. The loss of life attributed to this war and its resulting famine has reached catastrophic proportions, with the total counted as dead reaching numbers over two million. This is only an estimate, however, as we may never know the complete toll of this genocide.

Life as the people of Southern Sudan once knew it was coming to an end, just as "The Journey of the Lost Boys" was about to begin.

Nimeiri, furious over the defection of Garang and his renegade soldiers, ordered a killing spree in Dinka land. He justified the bloodshed of the innocent civilians under the guise that he was eliminating the SPLM/A from the South, offering the explanation that because Garang was a Dinka, all Dinkas were SPLM/A supporters. He attempted to disguise the civil war as one of inner tribal conflicts, enlisting the help of area tribes such as the Baqqara (later known as the Murahileen) to assist the GOS in their battle against the South.

19

The Baqqara, former neighbors of the Dinka, had often grazed and watered their cattle on Dinka land. The Dinka willingly shared their land and water with the Baqqara, knowing that it could one day jeopardize the well-being of their own livestock, but it was their custom to share with those in need. I use this statement in past tense because that philosophy is seldom practiced in Dinka land today. Not because of a change of heart on the part of the Dinka, but rather because in the aftermath of this current civil war, the Dinka no longer have anything of value to share.

Although the land and water belonging to the Dinka had once been a primary means of survival for the Baqqara and their livestock, it was now a secondary issue. The GOS, in an effort to compensate their low wages, gave the Baqqara the rights of ownership to anything confiscated during their raids on the Dinka. This not only included their food, possessions, and prized livestock, but also their women and children. The Baqqara, now armed by the powerful GOS, were sent with the blessings of the Sudanese government to murder, capture, and destroy the Dinka and their villages. Together, the forces of the North swept through the South with a vengeance, leaving a trail of blood and devastation behind them. Those who survived this crusade of death and destruction were often captured and sold into slavery, becoming the house servants and laborers to the Baqqara and Arab Muslims of the North. Some of these women and children (boys and girls alike) eventually escaped from their captors and returned with chilling stories of sexual and physical abuse at the hands of their Northern masters. There are also accounts of young boys who were sent to Islamic orientation schools, where they were forced to convert to the ways of Islam. Those failing to comply or attempting escape were reportedly beaten and bound in shackles. In some cases, they were killed and used as an example to the others. Those who submitted to their Arab captors, converting to Islam, were often enlisted in the GOS Army and sent back into the South with orders to kill their own people.

The young boys and men still remaining in the South, having escaped capture and death at the hands of GOS forces, were often recruited or reportedly captured by the SPLA and enlisted as soldiers in the fight against the North. Others say they willingly joined the rebel army as a duty to their people, even though they were young children at the time. The SPLA has long been accused of using underage boys in its army, but this accusation is a controversial one to say the least, one that Garang has reportedly denied in spite of conflicting reports from non-governmental agencies and former soldiers in the SPLA. When asking about this issue, the answers you receive will depend solely on the person(s) you are asking.

Those remaining survivors of the South, having lost their livestock and farmlands, were left without any means of survival and became displaced with

20

no place to call their home. These people, from various villages and regions, began the long and treacherous walk to bordering countries, such as Ethiopia, in search of refuge. They walked together by the hundreds of thousands, most of them children, the majority young boys. A scattered few remained with their parents, but most walked alone. In all, as a result of this continuing civil war in Sudan, an estimated 20,000 Sudanese children have become separated from their parents. Aid workers named the overwhelming numbers of unaccompanied male minors the "Lost Boys of Sudan," but they are quick to tell you they are not lost from God, only their parents.

The majority of these young boys settled in three different refugee camps just inside the border of Ethiopia. In order to reach these camps, they had traveled on foot without shoes, shelter, or clothing for approximately three months. They walked across deserts and mountains, often without food or water. They were sometimes able to find fruit hanging from trees or small puddles of muddy water, which they shared with the wild animals. Many became so thirsty that they drank their own urine to survive. For the most part, their diet consisted of leaves, bark, bugs, and mud, save the occasional feast of dead and decaying animals that they found along the way. Disease and parasites plagued their young bodies. They encountered wild animals such as lions and hyenas, which simply plucked them from their caravans and carried them away for their next meal. Many, after succumbing to a lack of food and water, simply fell by the wayside, becoming easy prey for the animals that stalked them night and day.

Others, unable to cope with their continuing hardships, fell into a state of helplessness. The loss and devastation that overshadowed these young boys became too much for some to bear. These children, having lost all hope, took matters into their own hands, choosing to end their lives rather than wait for the inevitable. They hanged themselves from trees, ate the berries of poisonous plants, or simply threw themselves into the currents of occasional passing rivers. There was little intervention from the others as they witnessed the last moments of their friends and loved ones. The boys simply continued on their journey, a journey that seemed to lead them on a path of misery and certain death. If they happened to speak of the dead, they did so only briefly, calling them the fortunate ones—fortunate because their suffering was over.

These young Sudanese boys had little in common with their fictional namesakes from the Peter Pan movie, except that they had also become separated from their parents and were left to fend for themselves. The Lost Boys of Sudan were definitely not living in a paradise called Never Land, and their story was no fairytale. It was the beginning of a reign of terror in the South of Sudan, a terrible nightmare in which there seemed no end.

These are the stories of some of those who survived, stories of cherished childhood memories, families, and communities that are no more.

AJAK ATEM AJOK

DINKA REGION

Atem slowly closes his eyes, creating a black veil to the outside world. He searches in the dark corners of his mind for the land he once called home. He searches across the oceans and beyond the stars for a glimpse of Africa.

Traveling back through time, he finds his homeland of Sudan and he smiles at the memory of its beauty. Once again he takes in the glorious view of the setting sun as it transforms dancing clouds into brilliant colors of red, orange, and yellow. They hang like huge balls of fire that burn to the ends of the earth.

The water buffalo move with the sound of thunder as they travel in large herds across the land. They stop at one of the many tributaries that flow from the Nile and cool themselves in its refreshing waters. Gazelles, deer, and antelope follow in their footsteps as they roam freely across the vast plains of the Upper Nile. There are no fences, only freedom for all that wander these lands. Freedom that would soon become a distant memory in the minds of the people who lived there.

For a brief moment in time, Atem returns in his mind to the village of his birthplace located in the Bor region of Sudan. Once again he is a young boy living with his family and friends in the Dinka village of Kiir, which means "river" in the Dinka language. Atem is not sure how the village acquired this name because it is not located in the vicinity of a river. Perhaps the villagers simply liked the sound of it, or better yet, chose its name to reflect the rivers of life that flowed through it. The Dinka tribe, the single largest ethnic group in Sudan, are a simple people living from the land and waters that surround them. Their skin is a deep shade of black like that of finely polished ebony gleaming in the

African sun. They greet you with a smile that extends from one side of their darkened face to the other. It shines like a beacon that welcomes all that behold it. But behind this outward gesture lies a fiery temper; one that is slow to surface, but fierce when called forth. And it is the memories of these people, his people, that Atem cherishes above all things.

Atem had four sisters and three brothers from his mother, and eighteen stepbrothers and eleven stepsisters from his father's other four wives. There were also numerous relatives who lived within the same village.

Families, as a rule, are very large in Sudan. This is true, in part, because men are allowed to marry more than one wife. Atem's father was no exception to this rule as he had five wives of his own. Using straw, mud, and cow dung he made numerous "tukuls" (pronounced *too-kools*) or huts to house his family. There was an open-door policy among the children and they moved freely from one tukul to the other.

Atem was particularly close to one of his second cousins named Abul. She was approximately nine or ten years of age and Atem was perhaps four or five. It was common practice in their village for the older children to care for the younger ones while their parents worked in the fields or went about their daily duties. Abul had been assigned the role of caregiver for Atem, and the two had formed a very close bond.

They spent their days playing games with their friends and family, and often traveled farther away from their village than they should have. In his last memory of Abul, they were playing the Dinka game "Adeir" in a nearby field. Adeir is similar to the game of ice hockey, only it is played on the warm and dusty earth with feet that are left unprotected by a lack of shoes. A small ball is chipped from wood and pushed by large sticks from one team's side to the other. It is an intense game that requires the full attention of its players.

Perhaps that is why no one noticed as the intruder made its way onto the field or was not seen as it lay camouflaged basking in the afternoon sun. Oblivious to its presence, Abul ran straight toward it as she played. Sensing danger, the Egyptian cobra raised its head in full crown and struck the young girl's legs, tearing the flesh as its large fangs pierced her skin. The poisonous venom spread quickly through her bloodstream, and her small body reacted immediately from its lethal dose.

She screamed in pain, and shortly thereafter began to vomit and foam at the mouth. Her body shook and jerked uncontrollably, as her breathing became difficult and labored. Within a short period of time her small body lay rigid and still. Frightened by the snake and uncertain of what to do with Abul, the young children quickly ran back to the village for help.

The elders of the tribe came running with spears, and without mercy, they killed the deadly cobra. The large snake hung from their pointed tips as it dangled in the air, stretching over six feet in length. The elders dropped the cobra to the ground where it lay lifeless and still, its final battle ending in defeat. Less than two hours later, in the village of Kiir, Abul took her last breath and her body also lay still. From that day forward, the young girl who had once been Atem's caregiver, cousin, and friend would live only in the hearts and minds of those who loved her.

Life continued to move forward for the remaining villagers—a life guided by the seasons and their harvests, a life filled with the Animist traditions of the tribal ancestors. Christian missionaries began infiltrating the South of Sudan in 1905, following the opening of the first mission in the region of Bor. However, many of the villagers who subsequently converted to Christianity continued to observe and participate in the Animist rituals of their ancestors.

Atem, who by now was six or seven years old, had just received his permanent teeth, thus making him eligible to participate in his first of these rituals. All tribal members were required to complete this ritual in order to receive their rights of initiation into the tribe. It was not a ritual that was relished or desired by most of the young boys and girls who were forced to participate. In fact, in their efforts to avoid the initiation process, many of the children developed a critical skill. They acquired, with much practice, the ability to run faster than a speeding bullet. This skill was necessary for those hoping to escape the tribal elders and the painful procedure that followed if captured. The ability to run with great speed would also prove to be essential in the years to come—when young children would be forced to run to save their lives.

Atem was playing with friends in the confines of the village and was caught off-guard as the tribal elders surrounded him. "I was just playing and having a good time," says Atem. "The tribal elders came to me and quickly grabbed me, leaving me no time in which to respond. They held me tightly as I was carried away. I was really scared because I knew something was up and I began to cry. They tried to reassure me, but spoke only lies, as they said, 'Don't worry, Atem. Everything is okay. You're a good boy. It's going to be alright.' As they held me tightly, one of the elders took a sharp instrument (similar to a small surgical knife) and positioned it between two of my lower middle teeth. He moved the knife forcefully back and forth between the teeth with all his strength. I was screaming and crying, but he continued to move the knife in this manner until the teeth were loose and pulled from their sockets." Depending on the tribe, at least four and up to six of the lower middle teeth were removed in this ritual. The elders went for the maximum with Atem on that day, removing all six of his lower middle teeth. "I was given nothing for the pain and it hurt really bad. I cried so hard," says Atem. "The blood was falling from my mouth."

There are numerous explanations for this ritual. Some say it is practiced for aesthetic reasons, and that those who remove their teeth are more pleasing to behold. Others say it is done to distinguish the different tribes. Atem does not believe it to be a ritual passed down by his ancestors, but rather a practice put into place by the Arabs of the North to distinguish their people from the tribes of the South. Separating the two, in order to further persecute the Southern Christians and Animists of the South. But in spite of his protest and personal doubts about the tribal roots of this procedure, it is a marking, none the less, that Atem now displays with each of his endearing smiles.

His completion of this ritual was also an indication that he was prepared to participate in other various duties performed by young men in the village. One of those duties included leaving the confines of the village and escorting the cattle on their long journey to the cattle camps. Cattle camps were temporary dwelling places where the villagers and cattle lived during the dry season of the year. "There was no predetermined day in which we left the village for cattle camp," says Atem. "The day and time were determined by the condition of the weather, and this changed from year to year. Sometimes the dry season came earlier than the year before and sometimes it came later. We just waited until the rains stopped."

When it became clear that the dry season was, in fact, on the way, scouts from each village were sent to the camps in advance to claim the best areas for their people. Located along the Upper Nile, the camps were in close proximity to the river, which was a priority for the villagers and the cattle. There were hundreds of sites to choose from, but the prized locations were those closest to the riverbank and those providing sufficient grass for the cattle to graze.

Once the scouts had selected and secured such a spot, they sent word for the other villagers to join them. Those too young or too old to travel would remain behind in the village along with the married elders and their wives. It would be their sole responsibility to protect and maintain the village while the others were away. Those who stayed behind were left with the task of preparing the fields for the returning cattle campers and the rainy season that would follow.

Those making the journey to the cattle camp (approximately 60% of the village) were generally young adults, who were not yet married, and children who were brave enough to leave the protection of their mothers. The younger children were not required to attend the camp, but if they did choose to go, they were placed in the care of older siblings or relatives and sent on their way. If after arriving they changed their minds, desiring to return to their parents, an older brother or relative escorted them back to the village. Depending on the ages, the elder children were often required to carry the younger ones on their backs or shoulders for the duration of the journey. This was no minor task, as the camps were sometimes a five-day journey from the village, and the only transportation was one's own feet.

I asked Atem what the young people did at cattle camp and he replied in a deep tone of reverence, saying "Cattle camp is a place where the children and young adults learn the ways of life, the values of society. The males are taught to wrestle in competitions in order to become strong warriors. It is a place where young boys learn how to become respectful young men." In hearing the tone and manner in which he speaks, I picture cattle camp as a no-nonsense place where the values of young people are shaped and molded through extensive and disciplined training. And this is a valid assumption on my part. But upon further questioning, Atem also casually mentions the fact that cattle camp, for the most part, is a place with little adult supervision, a place where young people generally follow the rules and regulations of their own making.

Suddenly, a much different picture begins to form in my own mind of the notorious cattle camps. I picture young people walking off into the African horizon, mindful of the fact that they will have little adult supervision for the next several months. I see them walking alongside the cattle in a responsible and orderly fashion until passing just beyond the sight and hearing range of their parents. And then a different demeanor begins to emerge, as their walking turns into the jumping of their native dances, and their voices rise in Dinka tongue shouting "Lour, Lour!" or "Let's party, Let's party!"

Granted, this is pure speculation on my part, as I have never witnessed the departure of African youths on their way to cattle camp. But I can't imagine that, even in the most remote parts of Africa, some things are not the same among the younger generations in our world. I share these thoughts with Atem and he erupts into a fit of laughter. His face looks like that of an American youth who has just been busted. (Meaning that they have told a story to someone, most likely an adult or parent, while intentionally withholding certain details that paint a much different picture when revealed. And then to the shock and embarrassment of the storyteller, the person(s) listening to their story begins to fill in the missing pieces, arriving at a much different conclusion of the story.)

With all pretense now left behind, a broader view of life in the cattle camps begins to unfold. After arriving at the pre-selected campsites, there was in fact much work to be done. In addition to the leisure activities and celebrations that made up cattle camp, the youths assumed responsibilities that previously fell on the shoulders of their parents and elders when living in their villages. Shelter was a priority, and the campers quickly set about the task of gathering straw and branches to build their temporary huts. Unlike the mud tukuls in their village, these temporary huts were much less durable and offered only minimal protection from the elements. The usual design was one that displayed a pointed straw roof supported by straw walls. Each group made their own huts, and the appearance and style varied according to the imagination of the creator. Some were square, others were round, and some were simply four straw walls with no roof at all.

With shelters completed and cattle contentedly grazing in the fields, the rhythm of the cattle camp began to pulse along the banks of the Upper Nile.

Cows' milk was the primary food source for the campers, and it was supplemented only with occasional grains such as sorghum, which is similar to wheat. When, and if, the grain supplies ran low, someone was sent back to the village for a fresh supply. The boys, in particular, needed to keep up their strength in order to meet the strenuous demands required of them in training for their wrestling and spear throwing techniques. They would need these skills in order to be successful in the competitions to be held among the various tribes living in the camps.

The boys needed to perform at their very best in order to beat the reigning champion from the previous year. "The title of champion brought honor to your family and tribe," explains Atem. "If you became champion, everyone would speak of your name. Songs would be sung and stories would be told in your honor." Then, Atem gets to the real significance of being named champion. "If you are named champion, you are considered to be of good breeding stock. All of the women, from miles around, will want to know you. You are placed in a position where you can choose any woman for your wife. Her father will be most happy to make a deal with you concerning her marriage. You could even pick more than one if you choose. If you are champion, you can pick as many women as you want," he says with a big smile. "All you must say is 'I pick this one, this one, and this one.' And they will be yours."

And the pickings were not slim, as thousands of people from various tribes and regions had come to settle in the temporary camps. There were hundreds of camps, some of them spanning over a five to ten mile radius. The people traveled frequently among the camps making new friends, visiting old ones from previous years, and exchanging news about the happenings in their villages. The young men, in particular, moved frequently from one camp to another, sizing up the competition and checking out the selection of available young women, just in case they earned the title of champion. Many of the young girls from the previous year had blossomed into very attractive women. At the sight of these beautiful young ladies, the young men gained new strength and inspiration for the coming competitions.

After much training and practice amongst their own tribe, the young men sent word to the various camps challenging other young men in a competition. All those willing to meet their challenge traveled to the appointed campsite on the predetermined day and time. The wrestling and spear throwing competitions usually lasted all day, sometimes continuing into the early evening. With the completion of the final match, a champion was named for that particular competition. Many competitions would be held in the months to come, and at the season's end, the final victor would be named the reigning champion of cattle camp.

These competitions were not like high school wrestling matches. They were serious business and often dangerous. "Many people were injured in these competitions," says Atem. "Sometimes their bodies would become broke." I asked, "Do you mean that they would have broken arms or legs?" He nods yes. I pushed on further, "Was there a doctor or a witch doctor in the camp to treat them?" He replies, "There was no doctor or a witch doctor. There were only regular people who could fix broken bones." I finished by asking "Where did they receive their training in such things?" Thinking for a minute, he says "I don't know." No one seems to know. "They just knew how to do it naturally! They treated everyone who became broken and then those people gave them a cow or traded something with them for their services." I assume that this is the Dinka version of the tribal HMO.

Wrestling matches were not the only events that took place in competitions, nor was it the only activity greeted with anticipation by the youth. When the fighting ended and evening began, a large celebration generally took place. "There was much dancing, even until the late hours of the night," says Atem. "It was a time for greeting the people and socializing. Everyone was happy and having a good time." I asked Atem if some of the older boys went on dates with girls while living in the cattle camp. His tone became very serious. "This is not permitted in our culture." I knew this to be true, but I also remember what it felt like to be a teenager and see a cute boy at a dance. "Do you think that some of them got together anyway?" I pressed. "I was very young at the time, but… yes, I think that maybe this happened." And then with a big grin, he begins to laugh out loud.

The courting process is not one that is taken lightly among the people of the Dinka tribe. If a young man wishes to pursue a relationship with an eligible young lady, he must do so in a manner that conforms to the strict guidelines enforced by the elders of the tribe and the girl's family. "A young man must never go to a girl's house without her prior permission to do so," explains Atem. "He must first ask the girl, 'Do you mind if I come to your house and visit you?'" If the girl agrees and permission is granted, a time and day are arranged for him to visit with her. This first date generally takes place outside the girl's home. The young couple sits on a mat in front of her parents' house, where they talk and get to know each other better. This is done in full view of the girl's family, but there is no talking or interaction between the boy and other members of her family. Her brothers and father will casually glance in their direction as they assess his worth as a suitor for their sister or daughter. After the young man has departed, they will ask her questions such as Whose son is he? and Where did he come from? If his background does not prove to be one of good lineage, they will not permit her to visit with him again. "If this happens," says Atem, "the next time you see her she will say to you 'I am very busy now' or 'I am not feeling very well.'" From this, I surmise that the proverbial "Not now, I have a headache" is an excuse that is apparently used by women from around the world, even by those living in the depths of rural Africa.

In many cases, the girl lives in a different village from her suitor, requiring him to travel several days on foot in order to reach his destination. It is often a difficult journey, one that he prays will not be in vain should she change her mind before he arrives. If the girl is a particularly good catch, the hopeful bachelor may find her visiting with another suitor upon his arrival. He may bump into yet another one on his way out. The girl holds the power to end her courting sessions at any time. If she makes a selection before receiving all of her scheduled suitors, the remaining young men are simply dismissed and told that she has made a selection. (But her choice is always subject to the approval of her family.) Without modern means of communication, these young men cannot be warned in advance should a change in events occur. They must first make the difficult journey to her house in order to receive the unfortunate news that their efforts have been in vain. Better luck next time!

Deviations from the rules of courtship can result in serious consequences. If a young man is caught alone with a girl without the permission of her parents or has in any way jeopardized her reputation, he may be faced with a life or death situation if her father and brothers find out! Atem explains, "If you are found in this situation, her brothers can make great danger for you." The actions of her brothers are not based solely on their deep love or devotion for their sister, or out of obligation to provide protection for her. It goes much deeper than that. The marriage of a daughter or sister is a matter of family honor as well as financial security and prosperity for her family. And it is a matter taken quite seriously by the male members of her family who will directly benefit from the payment of her dowry. The amount of her dowry is determined by her value, and that value is judged on the merits of her family's lineage, physical appearance, and virginity. Her perceived value drops considerably if her reputation has been tarnished in any way. In some cases, young boys are killed for such a violation, and it is done with the approval and blessings of the tribe.

Not only had Atem learned the basic rules for proper courting while living in the camps, he had learned many other new and exciting things as well—things that would help mold him into a respected member of his tribe. His first stay at the camp had truly been a memorable experience, one which he would never forget. But the dry season was coming to an end, and the first signs of rain began to appear, signaling the end of his stay at the camp. It would soon be time for Atem and the others to return to their respective villages. Atem was glad that he would soon see his parents once again, but he was also sad to leave the cattle camps behind. He would return to Kiir a much different person than the one who had left there only a few short months before. He had matured considerably during his brief time away from home, and he now held a new sense of pride regarding his role as a male member of his tribe. He looked forward to future years when he, too, would train as a warrior and compete in the many competitions held at the cattle camps. His thoughts were filled with dreams of becoming champion and of selecting many beautiful wives to bear his children. But like many of the children in Southern Sudan, Atem's dreams would never come true. This would be Atem's first and last stay at cattle camp. It was an experience that he both cherishes and remembers with great sorrow.

As the campers made preparations to return to their villages, a messenger appeared with alarming news from their homelands. He spoke fearfully and in excited tones as he described the terrible fighting that was taking place in the areas around their villages. This was not the typical tribal fighting that was fought with sticks and shields. This fighting came from the ground and the skies with loud explosions that destroyed entire villages. There were soldiers in great numbers marching on foot throughout the land. They were armed with powerful guns, and were seen shooting and killing men, women, and children at random. They ransacked villages, taking the livestock and anything of value, and then burned the remaining tukuls to the ground. The villages were left barren, ensuring their demise should any survivors return. The messenger urged them to flee from the area in order to protect themselves and their livestock. The people in the camps were frightened by the news, but leaving without first checking on their village was out of the question. It was decided that some of the younger children would return to the villages with the elders, while the older children fled with the livestock to a safer area.

Atem was chosen by his family to return with the others to look for his parents. If the fighting had not yet reached them, he must warn them to gather their belongings and flee to safety. After finding his parents, Atem was instructed to take them to a place where they would meet his older siblings, who were safely guarding the livestock. That meeting, however, would never take place.

Atem could see the fires in the distance as he approached his village. The sight comforted him at first because he thought his parents were just burning the previous season's crops. This was normally done at the end of the dry season in order to prepare the fields for the return of the campers and the new crops that were soon to be planted. Atem increased his pace as he ran excitedly toward his house to greet his parents. But as he drew closer to his village, the feeling of comfort was replaced with that of shock and horror. A feeling of loss and despair began to flood over him as he surveyed the remains of his village. "My village and everything in it were destroyed. The house of my family, along with everyone else's, had been burned to the ground. Dead bodies were scattered everywhere. There were so many bodies. Most of them were burned, and the smell was very bad." Atem speaks of this horrible smell while shaking his head back and forth and holding his fingers firmly pressed against both nostrils. These prove futile efforts on his part, to erase the smell of burning flesh or to

30

shake the painful images from his mind. For Atem, these are memories that will never be forgotten or erased.

Atem walked through the charred remains, searching for his parents or other members of his extended family. But due to the condition of the bodies, identification was almost impossible. An older man appeared from the bush where he had been hiding from the GOS soldiers and told him of the horrors that had taken place in their village. The old man had no words of encouragement for Atem in regards to the fate of his family. Atem felt a huge emptiness sweep over him as he tried to make sense of what had happened to them. The old man reached down to him and gently took him by the hand. Together they walked through the ashes and ruins of what had once been known as the village of Kiir. They moved forward in slow motion, leaving in their wake everything they once held dear. Their families, friends, and homes were now memories etched like deep scars in their minds. They walked not knowing where they were going or how long it would take them to get there. Atem's heart was heavy and ached from the tremendous loss. It seemed as if his life was hopeless and without meaning.

If only Atem could have looked into the future to another time and place, he would have seen a much different picture. He would have seen himself not as the helpless young boy of eight or nine years of age by the name of Ajak Atem Ajok. He would have seen himself as a young boy growing up to be a brave and courageous young man, a champion among his people. He would have seen himself as the man who became a Kiir: "the river of life" for his people.

ABRAHAM KUANY CHOL

DINKA REGION

Abraham was born in the village of Wernyol, located in the Upper Nile region of Southern Sudan. He lived there as a small child with his father, mother, sister, and two brothers. His five uncles and their respective families lived in a nearby village. Abraham and his relatives were members of the Dinka tribe, known for herding cattle and farming the land.

In this particular region of Sudan, tall grasses referred to as "the bush" cover the flat and desolate landscape. The height and density of these grasses serve as protective covering for the wild animals and tribal peoples who move within them, as well as for a variety of other uses among the villagers. The odd shapes of the acacia trees rise in bent and windblown patterns across the horizon. Their sparse and twisted branches struggle to shade the parched land beneath their shadows, as the sweltering African sun sparks new life into the freshly planted crops of the villagers. To those viewing this land for the first time, it may appear isolated and forsaken, a land without much value. But to Abraham and others like him who once called this land their homeland, its value is priceless.

Many of Abraham's childhood memories have faded with the passing of time, but the memory of his last day in Wernyol remains vivid and fresh. It is a day that Abraham says he will never forget. It began like many of the days before it with the cheerful singing of the first morning birds as they greeted the sleeping villagers, signaling the start of a new day. There was much to be done in the village during daylight hours, and an early start was essential.

The women were the first to emerge from the tukuls, beginning their day between the hours of 4 and 5 a.m. Their first chore of the day was to gather sufficient water for the daily cooking and cleaning of their tukuls. Depending on the geographic location of the village, the nearest river or watering hole may be a three to four mile distance. On rare occasions, a cow assisted the women in carrying the heavy load of water to the village. But this was typically a burden that the women alone were required to bear. In order to accomplish this difficult task, the women braided the soft leaves of nearby plants and trees or used tightly woven fabric forming it into long rolls. They then wrapped the rolls into tight rings and placed them on top of their heads. Large pots called "agulos," or similar containers, were placed on top of the rings in order to carry the water back to the village. The ring served as a resting place or cradle for the pots, helping the women to balance the heavy load and relieve some of the stress from their necks. This skill required many years of training that began when the women were small children.

Following their return to the village, the women set about the task of cleaning the vast amounts of dust that had collected in their tukuls from the previous day. It was a chore that must be done before the preparation of the morning meal. It was not uncommon for the men to leave the village before the women returned from the watering holes in order to begin working in the fields. In this case, the women simply delivered the completed meal to the men where they worked and assisted them afterwards if necessary. The women served the food in dishes they had made themselves by using gourds and clay. They made the gourd dishes by cutting the gourds in half, and then placing them in the river for approximately seven days until the inner meat had rotted. They then scooped out the rotten meat, letting the remaining shell dry in the heat of the sun until hardened. Milking jugs, used in milking the cows, were also made from the gourds. But for this purpose, only the tip of the gourds' long necks was removed. Long sticks were then used to puncture the meat deep within the neck and body of the gourd allowing the water to penetrate, and thus causing the meat to rot. After cleaning and drying the gourd, the long neck could be directly attached to the cow's nipple, preventing any loss of milk during the milking process. Milking the cows and churning the butter from the rich cream that floated on its surface was also a job performed primarily by the women of the tribe.

In making the clay dishes, the women used a mixture of mud and cow dung. They formed this clay into bowls and cups of various shapes and sizes and placed them in a pit that had been dug deep into the ground. Wood logs were placed on the bottom of the pit in an effort to make a floor where the dishes would be laid. Additional logs covered the top of the pit in an effort to seal it. Large mounds of grass were placed on top of these logs and set on fire. This created a tremendous heat as the fire burned down into the pit, creating a makeshift kiln. The final result was durable pottery, used by the villagers for eating and cooking their daily meals.

The women often decorated the gourds and pottery with various tribal designs. These designs were etched into the dishes by using pieces of cut wire that had been heated in fire and held by makeshift wooden handles. Peanuts were burned until blackened and rubbed into the crevices of the designs made in the gourds, thereby accentuating the markings. Oil was rubbed over the surface of the clay pottery to achieve the same effect.

The women, throughout the course of the day, prepared only two meals. Breakfast was usually served at 6 a.m., followed by dinner which was served around 6 p.m. Both meals generally began with a Dinka favorite called "Asida" or "Wal Wal," which the villagers consider bread. This particular bread was made from the grains of durra or sorghum, and had the consistency of raw dough that could be torn into small pieces. The remainder of the morning meal consisted of milk, beans, fried or boiled ostrich eggs (when available), salad (consisting of tomatoes, cucumbers, and onions), and on occasion, the liver of wild animals hunted by the villagers. Typically, dinner was the heartier meal of the two consisting of rich stews made from vegetables, grains, peanut butter (as a thickening agent), and meat. But in addition to using meats in stews, the villagers often prepared their meats in a variety of ways. Fresh meats were served smoked, boiled (such as in stews), or fried. Any excess meat was dried in a manner similar to that of beef jerky, highly salted and seasoned with spices. This allowed for storage of the meat without fear of contamination.

The men were primarily responsible for the hunting and skinning of the animals. They used the skins for a variety of purposes in the village, such as for clothing, blankets, and the musical instruments used in tribal dances and songs. It was not uncommon for the women to also participate in the hunting of wild animals, but this usually occurred only at the onset of the dry season. During this time of the year, large herds of animals, such as zebra, elephant, buffalo, gazelles and deer, moved through the forests and jungles surrounding the villages in search of water and new grazing grounds. The geographical location of each village determined what type of animals would be passing through that particular region.

The women, who were responsible for gathering the daily firewood, did so primarily in the jungles and forests where these herds of animals passed. The large sticks that they used in grinding their grains usually accompanied them. The women often came in close contact with the passing herds of animals and took every advantage of the opportunity. Hiding themselves in the tall grasses of the bush, the women stood patiently in wait. As the animals came within striking distance, they used large sticks to hit them in the head, pounding them until they were dead. These unfortunate animals were later served as the catch of the day on the Dinka dinner table.

Although the planting and harvesting of the crops were primarily the responsibility of the men, the cleaning and storing of those crops were left up to the women of the tribe. Following the cleaning process, the women placed the crops in what was called the store, a wooden hut built on stilts so that it was high above the ground. They covered the ground beneath it with cow dung in an effort to repel insects hoping to feast on the stored food. The villagers relied on these foods to sustain them during seasons when crops could not be grown.

There was much to be done in the daily routines of the villagers, and each person had a special job to do. At the end of the day as the hot sun began its descent and the cool evening air began to move through the village, the villagers who were tired and weary from a hard day's work looked forward to a time of rest and relaxation. This was the setting on Abraham's last day in the village of Wernyol.

Many of the men and young boys were returning from the countryside where they had been tending their livestock or working in their fields. Others who had spent their day hunting now returned with the fresh meat of antelope and gazelles. The women, finishing the last of their many daily chores, began the task of preparing the evening meal for their families.

The children, having also finished their allotted chores, were now busy doing what children around the world do best: They were playing. Abraham, who we estimate was six or seven years of age at the time, was too young to remember the exact game that he and his two brothers were playing. But he remembers that they were laughing and having a good time in a nearby field. Their fun was soon interrupted, however, by the sounds of gunfire coming from their village. Bap... Bap... Ba... Ba... Bap! The sounds of screaming and commotion followed. The gunfire grew louder and visibly closer as they witnessed bullets flying past their faces and landing in the dirt nearby. Abraham and his brothers did what would soon become an all too familiar ritual—they ran, each in a different direction. Everyone in the village scattered in a frantic attempt to escape the deadly bullets and the soldiers who fired them. What had begun as a typical day in Wernyol had now turned into a day of death, terror, and separation for the people who lived there. It was also the last day that Abraham would ever see his brothers, sister, or parents again.

GOS soldiers had invaded Wernyol leaving a killing field behind them. Abraham hid in the bushes for days waiting for the chance to return to his village and search for his family. Other boys who had also escaped joined Abraham where he hid and warned him not to go back. They told him that the soldiers were killing all males from the ages of two years of age and older. The soldiers did this to ensure that the young children would not fight against them in the rebel army. It was no longer safe for any of them to return to their village.

The mud and stick dwellings they called home were destroyed, and the people who once inhabited them had either been killed, were now missing, or were taken as slaves. That's right, slaves. Those of us living in America assume that the African slave market was abolished in the middle 1800s at the end of our own civil war. But make no mistake, the African slave trade is alive and prosperous. The total number of captives at any given time is estimated at 10,000 to 15,000. But the slave masters are no longer the greedy American landowners who once used African slaves to obtain their wealth. The slave masters of Sudan are none other than the victims' own countrymen. They are the extremist Arab Muslims of the North along with renegade tribes such as the Baqqara or the Murahileen. The years spent in civil war in the Sudan have been hard ones for those living in the South. "Too hard," Abraham whispers with his head hung low.

Abraham joined with others, mostly young boys who were also fleeing execution, and they began to walk. Their journey would be a long one, one in which they had no time to prepare. They had no food, water, or shelter, and no protection from the wild animals lurking within the bush, seeking their prey.

As GOS soldiers swept through Southern Sudan, many Sudanese found themselves in similar situations. These people would meet and walk together in groups. There was no longer a distinction between tribes or genders. In the face of death, those who were previously divided had now come together as one. They walked for approximately three months as they made their way east toward Ethiopia. Many walked without shoes or clothing to protect them from the elements. Most who walked were like Abraham, children who had become separated from their parents and families, many of whom had now become orphans. "I'm not sure what season it was because I was too young to remember," Abraham says. "But it was very hot and dry. It must have been summer (dry season). Yes, it had to be summer because there was no rain. There had been no rain for a very long time. We had not eaten in many days, and sometimes even if we happened to find something to eat, we didn't wish to because there was no water to drink. We were so thirsty that we sometimes drank our own urine just to survive. We were so tired and hungry that we began to feel defeated. It seemed as if all our hopes were gone and so we began to give up. There was nothing else to do at this point but stop and wait. We stopped and waited... for our time to die. But then it came to us without warning. It was a miracle for sure. As we waited for death to take us, the skies opened and rain poured from the heavens. We were jumping and shouting! Everyone was so happy because we couldn't believe it. It was raining! I lay down and let the rain wash over my body, and I shouted to God, 'Oh God, you really are there and you are watching over your people!' I knew at that time that if I died tomorrow, someone had, in fact, been looking over me and taking care of me. I knew this one hundred percent."

Many of the Lost Boys use drawings to depict attacks on their villages by GOS Forces.

by John Yok

by Deng Deng Koch

37

Joan Hecht ©2005

Even though I walk through the valley
of the shadow of death,
I will fear no evil,
For you are with me;
Your rod and staff
They comfort me.

Psalms 23:4

ETHIOPIA:
A PLACE OF REFUGE

E scaping death at the hands of GOS forces, or starvation due to the loss of crops and resulting famines, Abraham and Atem joined with other villagers fleeing the South of Sudan. Their small caravans soon grew into larger ones, swelling to numbers in the hundreds of thousands as they rolled across Ethiopian borders like a human tidal wave, flooding area refugee camps and sending shock waves amongst relief workers caught totally unprepared for the mass exodus. In their wake was left an indescribable path of death and destruction. Roger Winter, former director for USCR (U.S. Committee for Refugees), recalls the comments made by relief workers flying over the scene of carnage. "The path of the refugees is an easy one to trace," recalls Winter. "All one has to do is follow the trail of bones and bodies left scattered on the ground behind them."

Those managing to complete the long and grueling journey were sick, starving, and near death upon their arrival to Ethiopia. Many, who initially appeared to have survived the perilous walk, were in such a weakened state that they perished soon after reaching the camps. Negussie Tesfa was the regional coordinator for four of the refugee camps in Ethiopia during that time, hosting over 385,000 Sudanese refugees. Upon seeing the unaccompanied male minors, or Lost Boys, for the first time, he remembers them as being half naked and in very bad condition due to the long walk and lack of food along the way. It was a sight that few observers could ever forget.

Atem remembers meeting a U.S. Senator shortly after arriving in Ethiopia. "He (the Senator) just looked at us and started sobbing," says Atem. "He cried so hard that he couldn't speak any words to us. He just covered his face with his hands and cried many tears, for a really long time."

For the most part, the boys were placed in three separate camps along the Ethiopian and Sudanese border: "Dimma," "Itang," and "Pugnido." They were

40

assigned to these camps according to their points of entry into the country. They were separated into boys-only areas in the camps, and then divided again according to their tribes and ages into separate groups called "peer" groups.

And while it is true that most of the unaccompanied male minors fled from Sudan in an effort to escape death and persecution by the GOS militia, others were reportedly lured there by the SPLA, for the purpose of military training. In fact, there were numerous boys among the first groups to flee Sudan who had not been separated from their parents due to GOS attacks on their villages. They had instead been willingly handed over to the SPLA by their parents, with the assurance that they would receive food and an education while living in the camps. However, this was a promise that the SPLA, for the most part, fell short on delivering. The parents had also hoped that their children would be trained for combat by the SPLA and armed with guns and ammunition, so that they could better defend themselves during the attacks by GOS soldiers. Many of the parents felt that this was their only option for preserving family bloodlines and ensuring the continuation of their family name for future generations. As the mother of small children, the thought of using them as soldiers both saddens and sickens me. But in a country such as Sudan, where almost every day is like that of September 11, 2001, in America, with millions of innocent people being killed while the rest of the world looks idly by, I find it hard to criticize the actions that were taken by those parents.

Reportedly, foreign aid workers claimed to have heard the sounds of artillery coming from inside the refugee camps in the late afternoon and early evening hours, leading them to believe that the underage boys were receiving military training at this time. Those reports have been difficult to substantiate, however, as the Ethiopian government denied inside access to any foreign aid workers after the hours of five or six o'clock in the afternoon. The only exception to the rule was that extended to the Ethiopian nationals working with relief agencies inside the camps, and the nuns from Mother Theresa's organization, "Missionaries of Charity." As an Ethiopian national, Tesfa not only resided in the camps but was also granted access inside them, twenty-four hours a day. He suggests that perhaps the aid workers making these claims were not in the real picture as he had been, and assures me that no military training took place in Pugnido or any of the other camps. He says that such military training most likely occurred in "Bonga," an SPLA military base, located some 92 miles from Pugnido. However, the only SPLA presence that Tesfa recalls seeing inside of Pugnido was that of a small contingency of soldiers left in place to guard the family members of high-ranking SPLA officials who were living inside the camp, along with the sick and the wounded. And the only sounds he remembers coming from inside the camps during the early evening hours were those of the boys as they sang. Tesfa says, "Their voices drifted in beautiful melodies across

41

the evening air as they sang in the various tongues of their native tribes." Unfortunately, he was unable to decipher their numerous dialects and says that he has no idea what they were singing about.

The boys that I questioned agreed with Tesfa for the most part, saying that even though they had been recruited by the SPLA while living in the camps, they had been moved to other locations (like Bonga) for their actual military training. Their stories differ slightly in regards to Dimma, however, where some of them tell me that military training was mandatory for all unaccompanied minors 12 years old and up. This training reportedly took place just outside the main confines of the camp. When I asked if they had been forced to fight by the SPLA, Lost Boy William Wol Yol said, "They could not force us to fight because we were still too young. But if we chose to do so on our own, then they did not stop us." William says he joined the ranks of the SPLA at the tender age of 15, whereupon his AK-47 became his constant friend and companion."

Many of the Lost Boys from the Nuer region were placed in the "Itang" (pronounced E-tang) refugee camp, while the majority of the others were placed in the Dimma (pronounced Deem-Ah) and Pugnido (pronounced poogneed-o) camps. Of the three camps, Pugnido hosted the largest number of unaccompanied minors, with approximately 10,000 of the Lost Boy population of that camp hailing from the Dinka tribe, the largest tribe in residence. Because of the vast numbers of boys living in this camp, it will be the primary focus for this chapter.

Pugnido is located in the southwestern part of Ethiopia in the Gambella region. It is close in proximity to the small town of Panyido (pronounced panyee-dough) and is often referred to by that name. This is also the name by which most of the Lost Boys refer to the camp. But it is called by several other names as well, such as Pan-Ni-Do (a variation of the name Panyido) and Fugnido (Foog-nee-dough). The latter is most inaccurate, however, as there is no letter "f" in the Nilotec (Sudanese) dialect. Nevertheless, all names reference the same camp with the correct name being "Pugnido," which is taken from the dialect of the local people in that area called the "Anuaks." Pugnido, in the Anuak dialect, means "the land of the ostrich." Its name is an easy one to understand, as a large number of ostrich are said to flock to that area at the onset of the rainy season. One of the boys told me that the birds were a very curious sight to behold, as they gathered in vast numbers across the barren landscape, stretching as far as the eye could see. However, he was appalled when I asked him if they ate the birds and assured me that "they most certainly did not!" He did say however, "that the large eggs produced by the birds were a prized food source for those fortunate enough to find them."

The climate is very hot in Pugnido, similar to most of the areas in Sudan where the boys had lived previously. But the similarities stopped there, as

Pugnido in no way felt like home to these lost and abandoned young boys. The local administrator of Gambella, in conjunction with the UNHCR, initiated emergency relief operations within the camps, receiving assistance from such organizations as the Ethiopian Red Cross Society, Save the Children Foundation, Missionaries of Charity, World Food Program, and other Non-governmental organizations (NGOs).

Initially, shelter and housing were not provided for the boys, and the building of such structures, along with other necessary structures, became their sole responsibility. The smaller children did their part by collecting grasses and branches from nearby forests to be used in thatching the huts, while the older boys collected wood and larger sticks that were used in the actual design and construction of the structures. This was not a chore for which the boys eagerly volunteered, but rather one that was required of them by the "elders," those placed in charge of overseeing them and ensuring that their daily tasks were completed. I was told by one of the boys that anyone refusing to comply with an elder's orders was subjected to punishment by "Uncle Black." This was a name given to the whips that were used by some of the elders when administering punishments to the boys. The name for the whips was derived from the fact that the boys often referred to the elders as "Uncle," even though they were not blood relatives. And the word "black" came from the black rubber from old tires abandoned by relief workers, which was then shredded and attached to sticks. With the assistance of "Uncle Black," the elders achieved maximum compliance from the young boys, as they set about the laborious task of building their tukuls and other structures that made up Pugnido.

Upon completion of their tukuls, the boys were divided into different groups of about 30 boys per tukul. The tukuls were grouped into clusters, forming separate units consisting of approximately 150-175 children. Each group was headed by an adult caregiver who often functioned as a teacher. Some were actually qualified teachers, but most had no formal training whatsoever. They were simply literate people who had been chosen from among the adult refugee population in the camp. A rudimentary health service was also established, with the assistance of a Sudanese doctor and several nurses who were also found living among the refugees in the camp.

A portion of the Gilo River flowed near the camp, and the boys regularly swam, bathed, and fished in its waters. Some even grew small gardens near the riverbanks, reaping meager harvests for their efforts. However their primary food source, grains and oil, came from the various relief agencies working inside the camp. Motorized grinding mills were unavailable for the majority of the time the boys lived in Pugnido, requiring the older boys to assist the younger ones in pounding the grains to produce flour or maize. To complete this task, the boys hollowed the end of a small log and poured the grains into

43

the hole. Then they pounded the grains with a large stick, its end whittled into a rounded tip. The use of wooden pestles and mortars made from area trees, such as the Acacia, was another method the boys used in pounding the grain.

Preparing the food was a difficult and time-consuming chore, one that had usually been performed by the women of their tribes. But the Lost Boys would assume many new roles in the days, months, and years that they would live in Pugnido. Roles they would be required to perform in order to survive. For many, in spite of their best efforts, it would be their final performance.

In spite of the safe refuge allowed them while living in Pugnido, the lives of the boys continued to be difficult at best. In fact, Atem tells me that the worst experience of his journey occurred shortly after his arrival to Pugnido. He said that he and several of his friends journeyed to the river one day, as they often did, for a cool and refreshing swim. On the way, they spied their best friend Maluak lying on a mat in his tukul. They called for him to join them, but Maluak waved them on, complaining that he wasn't feeling well, saying that he didn't have the strength to make the long walk. The nearest river was approximately a mile from the camp, and in the weakened condition of the boys it was not unusual for one of them to decline the strenuous journey. So without hesitation, Atem and the other boys waved back to their friend and continued on their path to a fun-filled day at the river. Later that afternoon, when returning from the river, they found their friend lying in the same spot in which they had left him earlier that day.

Realizing that he must be feeling worse than they had initially thought, they approached his tukul to see if they could be of any assistance. To their surprise, they found Maluak dead, his body stiff and cold. Atem estimates that Maluak was approximately seven or eight years old at the time. The young boys felt consumed by guilt for having left their friend to die alone, but with nightfall fast approaching there was nothing else they could do except wait for morning to bury him. The next day, using a makeshift shovel, the young boys took turns digging the grave. It took them approximately seven hours to complete the task. Atem's eyes fill with tears as he recounts this story, and his Dinka temper flares at the memory of his young friend's death. "This is something that you do not read about in history books," he says. "In all the wars throughout time, you have not heard of such things—children burying children. It is for this reason that I will never become a friend of the Muslims. Even in times of peace, I will not be their friend."

In addition to the relief efforts that were provided by the various missionaries living in the camp, religious instruction was also offered as well. For the most part, their teachings followed those of the Catholic and Episcopal churches, and under the missionaries' tutelage, many of the young boys converted to Christianity and were subsequently baptized. Following those baptisms, they were given the option of choosing new Christian names in addition to the names given to them by their parents. Typically they selected from among Biblical names such as Simon, Gabriel, Abraham, Peter, and so forth. However, since the large volume of boys far outnumbered the pool of names they had to choose from, many were forced to select the same names. As a result, you can generally greet a group of the boys with, "Hi, Peter" or "Hello, Simon" and most likely receive a response from at least one of them, making the task of remembering their names a much easier one. But some of the boys refused the new Christian names, fearing that their families would be unable to locate them upon returning to Sudan. These boys remained hopeful that their families were still alive, praying fervently for peace in their homeland while dreaming of the day they would be reunited.

But peace was nowhere to be found in the Sudan. During the four years that the boys lived in Ethiopia, the Sudanese government moved in a downward spiral under the leadership of numerous rulers who proved to be both corrupt and incompetent in their reigns. Any hopes of achieving peace during this period were quickly dispelled.

In 1985, while visiting the U.S., Nimieiri was overthrown in a military coup led by his Chief of Staff, Lieutenant General Siwar-al-Dahab, and subsequently exiled to Egypt. Dahab moved quickly to dismantle the former civil service and secret police, creating instead the Transitional Military Council (TMC) to assist in the newly formed government. Hundreds of political prisoners were released at his command, and immunity was granted to the rebel soldiers. Following his order for a cease-fire, Dahab was able to establish direct communications with the SPLA, and promised them that he would seek a resolution to the civil war. But any attempts on his part to negotiate such a resolution quickly collapsed at his refusal to banish Sharia law.

Following a one-year period, Dahab relinquished control of the Sudanese government, turning it over to civilian rule as was originally promised. He was only too happy to do so as the country lay in financial ruins, with no end to the civil war in sight. But any attempts at a civilian rule in Sudan were doomed before they ever began. Under the leadership of Sadiq Al Mahdi, the civilians were also unsuccessful in their attempts to reduce the country's debt, or in ending the longstanding war. Sadiq's only glimmer of success came in 1988 when he placed a temporary freeze on Sharia law following a signed agreement with the SPLA in Addis Ababa. Unfortunately, that agreement, like the Addis Ababa Peace Treaty of 1972 before it, collapsed under the constant pull between North and South. Any praise earned by Sadiq was quickly forgotten when, after promising to deliver food to the areas in the South hardest hit by drought and famine, hundreds of thousands died waiting for that food to arrive. Sadiq, like his predecessors before him, was also decried a failure.

It was for these reasons, along with the prospect of a successful peace agreement with Southern Rebels, that in 1989 Sadiq was overthrown in a fundamentalist-based military coup led by Colonel Omar Hassan Al Bashir. Bashir, secretly supported and funded by the NIF (now under the direction of Hassan Al Turabi), moved quickly to re-establish Islamic rule in Sudan, and to assist him in that task, he formed the Revolutionary Command Council for National Salvation. Civilian rule was brought to an end and with it the current constitution and remaining political institutions.

The new government of Sudan, now under the influence and control of the NIF, became a police state, and its military became the driving force behind the NIF'S mission to eliminate the Southerners. However, in spite of the overwhelming manpower and modern weaponry of the GOS, the Southern rebels continued to gain ground. By all accounts and observations, the rebels appeared to be succeeding in their struggle against the powerful North, or at the very least, holding their ground. But that was all about to change…

ABRAHAM GARANG AJAK

DINKA REGION

The journey from Sudan to Ethiopia had been a long and hard one, a journey filled with fear, suffering, and sorrow for the small children like Abraham who had lost everything they had ever held dear.

Abraham began his journey in the village of Alian, located in the Bor region of Southern Sudan. GOS soldiers raided his village at night, causing him to become separated from his mother, father, and siblings. He estimates that he was approximately seven years old at the time. (You may have noticed that I often refer to the ages of the boys in estimated years. I do so because the major-ity of the Lost Boys do not know their exact ages. In fact, most were so young when they were separated from their parents that they have no knowledge of the day or year in which they were born.)

As was customary, the children of Abraham's village often ate their evening meals with relatives of their own age, alternating nightly between the various homes. On this particular night, it was around 7 p.m. and Abraham was eating at the home of his uncle with his "equal" (same age) cousin Deng Arou. But their dinner was soon interrupted by the sound of gunshots and screaming. They quickly ran outside to see what the commotion was all about and found villagers running frantically in all directions. Strange men ran behind them, shooting at the villagers—men, women, and children—as if they were wild ani-mals. Abraham began screaming in fear and shouted to his uncle, "Who are these people shooting at us?" His uncle replied, "Wow, these are the Arabs. They have come because we worship God in our own way! They want to kill us and burn this place. You must run, Abraham. You must run now! Run!"

Abraham ran quickly to his home in search of his parents, but he found his

47

house to be empty. His heart sank in fear at the realization that his family had already fled without him. Abraham turned and ran alone into the darkness, with tears falling from his eyes he called for his mother and father. "Mama, Baba (Papa)," he called to them over and over again, but his calls were never answered.

Eventually, Abraham came upon an old man who was walking with his own family. The old man asked, "Who are you? Where have you come from, child?" Abraham told him about the attack on his village, explaining that he was lost from his family and walking all alone. The old man took pity on Abraham and invited him to join them as they walked toward Ethiopia. Abraham traveled with the man and his family for approximately three months before they reached the safety of Pugnido Refugee Camp. However, upon their arrival to Pugnido, they were forced to separate. The old man and his family were assigned to an area of the camp designated for refugee families, while Abraham, without a family of his own, was assigned to an area that housed unaccompanied male minors.

Before parting, the old man took Abraham to a group of his "peers" and instructed them by saying, "You must always stay together and look after one another." But these words brought little comfort to Abraham because he had grown close to this man and his family, who for many months now had treated him as one of their own. Once again, Abraham felt abandoned and began to cry at the thought of being left alone again. The old man tried to console him saying, "Maybe your parents will come for you, Abraham; maybe they will not. But no matter what you do, don't give up hope. Keep hoping that your family is still alive." And with that, the old man and his family turned and walked away.

As Abraham walked to his assigned area of the camp, his heart was filled with the hope that his parents and family were still alive. But that night when he closed his eyes, he saw the people of his village once again as they fell from the enemy's gunfire. He heard their desperate screams carried by the night air. "Help me, I've been shot! Oh God, I'm going to die!" He saw the frightened faces of the villagers, their bodies crumpled on the ground, as they closed their eyes for the very last time. Abraham cried himself to sleep that night, while aching for the sound of his parents' voices and wondering about their fate. This became a nightly ritual for Abraham, one that he would practice for many years to come.

"There was no food for at least two weeks when we arrived in Pugnido," says Abraham. "I was so hungry that I didn't know what to do. One day, I was walking to the river for a drink of water and I saw something on the ground. I picked it up and saw that it was a rusty needle with a piece of thread running through it. I took the needle and placed it into the fire until it became hot. I banged on it with a stone until I bent it in the shape of a hook, and then I dug up worms from the muddy riverbank and put them on the hook to get the attention of the hungry fish. I placed the hook and thread into the river and soon after-

48

wards, I snagged a fish, but it slipped from the hook and fell back into the water. Once again I put the hook into the river catching a fish, and once again the fish fell from the hook splashing back into the water. But I refused to give up because I was very hungry, so I tried again and again. And then the third and fourth fish... they stayed! I ate those fish," says Abraham, "and they were really good!"

Although the fish provided temporary nourishment, it would not be enough to ward off the constant hunger, or the sickness and disease that would follow. Abraham became ill soon after his arrival to Pugnido, and was taken to a makeshift hospital constructed of mud with a thatched roof. "There were so many people in such a small place," says Abraham. "There was sickness everywhere." The number of sick and starving people who arrived each day was staggering, and their bodies began to pile one upon the other in the overcrowded hospital.

Abraham contracted what he believes was measles and was given medication to treat it. However, he is not sure what type of medication he received. Some of the boys tell me that they were often given aspirin, even for the most serious of conditions. One boy told me that while living in the camps, the only medication he ever received for his severe hepatitis was aspirin. This was probably because it was the only medicine available. And of course, even a simple aspirin was quite an improvement over the treatments they had received while living in their villages in Sudan. The tribal witch doctors in their villages typically treated someone with measles by cutting a "V-shaped" pattern into his forehead. The deep cuts caused considerable bleeding, which in turn was said to have broken the patient's fever and cured the measles. Some of the boys I've spoken with received such treatments, evident by the scars on their foreheads, and they were cured without any additional means of treatment. Of course, given the choice, I strongly feel that these boys would have opted instead for the aspirin!

Abraham says he was given a pill each morning with a tiny sip of water, and then once again in the evening with another sip of water. There would be no food or water in between. "This sickness caused you to be so thirsty," Abraham says. "Some people would drink a lot of water thinking it would make them feel better. But this is when the end began, because drinking the water would cause the diarrhea, and then came the end."

The end would come for many in Pugnido. Abraham remembers waking in the hospital every day and being surrounded by death. "Every morning I opened my eyes and someone would be lying dead beside me. I wanted to leave that place so badly. I told myself that no other place could be this bad. The nurses told me that if I became able to stand up and walk that I would be allowed to return home to my tukul. Each day I tried to do this, but I was too weak and unable to complete the task. One day I stood up and after taking a few steps I called to the nurses, 'Look, I am walking!' They told me that if I was strong enough to walk out of the hospital that I could leave that place, and that is what I did. I was very weak and it was hard to do, but I took a few steps and then stopped under a tree to rest in the shade. After a while I would walk another short distance, and then once again lie beneath a tree to rest. I had to walk a very long way, but I just kept going no matter what until I finally made it!"

Abraham returned home to his tukul made of mud and twigs, crowded with the young boys he now called brothers. And in spite of the hardships that Abraham was forced to endure while living in Pugnido, life was good because there was school, medication, food, and a roof over his head. And unbeknownst to Abraham, life in Pugnido was about to get a whole lot better.

Abraham had been living in Pugnido for approximately three years when a familiar face walked into the camp one day calling to him by name. *Surely this is a dream! This cannot be real*, thought Abraham. But the person walking toward him was not a dream—it was instead his older brother, Peter. Peter ran excitedly to Abraham, picking him up and tossing him into the air. "There was a lot of hugging and crying that day," Abraham says with a smile.

Peter was at cattle camp when their village had been raided, thus being one of the more fortunate ones to have been spared. But he, like Abraham, was also uncertain about the fate of their parents and sisters, and after remaining in Pugnido with Abraham for only one year, they both decided that Peter should return to Sudan and search for their family. Before leaving, Peter promised Abraham that he would return someday with their family, or with word of their demise. But his promise would be broken, as civil war erupted in Ethiopia soon after Peter's departure. Once again, Abraham had become separated from his family, and with the sound of gunfire ringing in his ears, he went alone into the future, uncertain of his family's fate and that of his own. He called out to God, with one simple request: "Please dear God, let me live so that I may be a future for my family."

JOHNSON MAYIEL KUETH

NUER REGION

ohnson had been standing in line for over an hour at Pugnido, waiting for his daily food rations. He knew the menu in advance, because it would be the same today as it was yesterday and every other day: grains. But the constant groaning of his empty belly forced him to remain in line, even though the hot afternoon sun burned with such intensity that it scorched his skin and caused his throat to become parched and dry.

After what seemed an eternity, Johnson's turn finally arrived, and as predicted, he received two cups of sorghum, two cups of corn, and one cup of oil for cooking the grains. The oil was to be shared with all the boys living in his tukul. And although the small portions of grain were the only rations he would receive for the entire day, Johnson was appreciative nonetheless. There had been times when rations ran extremely low and there would be no food served at all, sometimes for several days. In addition to the grains and oil, the boys also received two to five cups of water when available. However, the number of people waiting in line each day determined the actual amount given, as it often varied. Many days there were fewer children in line than the day before, and the reason for the decline was not a difficult one to figure out. You see in spite of the safe refuge allowed them while living in Pugnido, deaths among the youths continued to climb, as starvation and disease took their toll upon their young bodies.

After receiving his paltry rations, Johnson began the long trek back to his tukul in order to prepare his meal. At nine or ten years of age, he was considered one of the older boys among his group and was therefore responsible for grinding his own grains and preparing his meals. Johnson accomplished this task with the assistance of a large mortar that was used to pound the grains. This was normally the responsibility of the mothers, sisters, and grandmothers of his tribe and was considered humiliating work for a man, but his pride must now be put aside since the alternative was much worse. Refusing to prepare his own food would have sealed Johnson's fate because without any women of his tribe to help him, he would have surely starved to death. Yes, it was a difficult and time-consuming task, but time happened to be the one thing the boys had to spare.

Each day they gathered kindling from the nearby forest to be used in building small fires to cook their meals. After pounding the grains, the resulting flour was mixed with a portion of their allotted water, and then cooked in small pots hanging above the fires. The boys were allowed only one small pot per tukul, and there was never enough food to fill even that one pot.

Johnson's tukul consisted of four mud walls covering an area of roughly seven by seven feet, covered by a thatched roof. He shared the tukul with three other Lost Boys by the names of Joseph, Ezekiel, and Tut (pronounced Toot). The four had come from the same region in Southern Sudan, and as a result, they shared many things in common. Johnson and Joseph were actually blood relatives, which was a rare luxury in the camp as most boys had become separated from all members of their family. And although these young boys had little in the way of personal possessions, they were comforted by the fact that they had each other. As a result, Johnson and Joseph formed a strong bond that would link them together for the rest of their lives. They became "brothers," vowing to love and protect each other forever.

Initially, the peasant lifestyle of Pugnido was a difficult adjustment for Johnson as he had come from a wealthy family, according to tribal standards. His father had been very affluent and respected among his tribe, owning large fields that were rich in minerals and flourishing with crops of sorghum, corn, beans, and onions. In addition to their bountiful crops, his family also owned large amounts of livestock. "We had forty sheep, twenty-one goats, and too many cows to count," says Johnson. "I think we had 4,000 cows," he recalls proudly. (It may seem inconceivable for a young child of nine or ten years old to remember the number of livestock his father owned so many years ago, but when understanding the significance of these animals, it's not surprising at all.)

Although the cows and livestock provided the villagers with milk, meat, and barter power for purchasing crops and needed supplies, they also played a significant role in various tribal ceremonies. For instance, at the birth of each child, a special ceremony was held presenting each child with their very own head of cattle. Male children were given a bull or ox while females were given a cow. The middle name of the children often reflected certain characteristics of their animals, such as their color. Johnson's middle name, Mayiel, means orange and white cow—the colors of the bull given to him at birth. Each child in a family was given an animal of differing colors. The care of these cattle became their sole responsibility when coming of age, and the cattle could not be sold, traded, or sacrificed without the child's permission, regardless of their ages.

Cows and livestock were not just important for the prestige and power that came with owning them. They were also of great value because of their bartering power when purchasing brides for the father and sons of the tribe. As mentioned previously, not only is it not uncommon it is rather the norm to have more than one wife in rural Africa. In addition to the father of the bride, it is customary to pay a dowry of cows to the brothers and grandfather of the bride as well. Depending on the tribe, you may be required to pay up to 150 cows per bride. Johnson's father had three wives and fourteen children—nine of which were girls! That adds up to a lot of cows!

On the day that war broke out in his village, Johnson's mother and father were working in the fields. He and his brother, Nygon, were playing in their straw tukul. Since he was only nine or ten years old at the time, Johnson is not sure of the whereabouts of his sister, Naikoul, his brother, Pourk, or the members of his stepfamily. "It was early morning and the soldiers came on foot. There were too many to count. They also came in helicopters shooting from the sky. My brother and I ran from our hut in the same direction, but soon became lost in the crowd of people who were also trying to escape. I was running as fast as I could in hopes of catching up with him when suddenly the two people in front of me were shot and killed from the sky. They fell to the ground and died right before my eyes. I jumped to miss them and began running in a different direction in an effort to escape from the helicopters," he recalls. "There were bodies falling everywhere, but my only concern was trying to survive. And that is how I became separated from Nygon—he went one way and I another." In the weeks and months that followed, Johnson would run to the shelter of two distant villages. Enemy soldiers followed close behind, intent on hunting and killing this young boy and others just like him. Fortunately, this was one mission the soldiers would fail.

After months of running from enemy soldiers, with little food or water, Johnson reached Pugnido. Although he was relatively safe there, each day was overshadowed by the uncertainty of his family's fate. Four years after his arrival, however, Johnson received some much welcomed news regarding his brother. Apparently Nygon had also reached Ethiopia and was currently living somewhere inside Pugnido. And while it may seem impossible that their paths had never crossed, one must keep in mind that there were hundreds of thousands of refugees living within the confines of this camp. Finding his brother could prove as difficult as finding a needle in a haystack. But Johnson was determined to reunite with his lost brother, and he had just begun the overwhelming process of finding him when civil war broke out in Ethiopia, forcing him to flee the country, separating him from his brother once again. Separating them this time forever.

Before leaving Pugnido, however, Johnson did receive word about the fate of his parents. He was told that in the aftermath of the raid on his village, his mother and father were found shot and lying dead in their luscious fields—the fields of dreams and success for their family. However, they did not lie alone that day, because the hopes and dreams of their children lay with them.

Boys in tent at Pugnido

Boys grinding grain

55

The Journey of a Thousand Miles
by Awer G. Bul

ESCAPE
FROM ETHIOPIA

On December 25, 1991, at 7 p.m., Mikhail Gorbachev addressed the Soviet Union for the last time as President of the U.S.S.R., announcing his resignation. Six days later, the U.S.S.R. ceased to exist under the guidelines of international law, marking the end of the cold war. The complete totalitarian rule of socialism and fascism in the Soviet Union came to a halt as the Iron Curtain fell with a crash heard round the world.

Some of those suffering the greatest impact from that fall were the countries and regimes previously supported both financially and militarily by the former communist government. Many of those countries now found themselves in dire straits economically and, without military assistance from the Soviets, were completely vulnerable to their enemies. One such country was Ethiopia, whose ruler Mengistu Haile Mariam watched helplessly as his empire crumbled before his eyes and his enemies rose in great numbers against him.

Mengistu had long battled with the predominantly Muslim Eritrean rebels, known as the Eritrean Peoples Liberation Front (EPLF), who lived in an area to the north of Ethiopia called Eritrea. The Eritreans sought to regain their independence, which had been taken from them by former Ethiopian Emperor Haile Selasie. In an effort to achieve this goal, they formed an alliance with the predominantly Christian Tigrayan rebels, known as the Tigrayan Peoples Liberation Front (TPLF), whose goal was to gain control of the Ethiopian government. Together, the two rebel factions, along with others who later joined them, moved across Ethiopia in a united force.

The Sudanese refugees, particularly the Lost Boys living along the Ethiopian border in the refugee camps of Dimma, Itang, and Pugnido, were assumed by the new government to be supporters of Mengistu and the SPLA and subsequently ordered to leave the country. They were given only days in

58

which to comply. While those living in the camps began immediate preparations for their departures, those in Bonga (the camp used by the SPLA for the military training of the unaccompanied minors) met thoughts of evacuation with extreme reluctance. Not only had Bonga been a training site for future SPLA soldiers, the camp had also served as a storage compound for the large cache of arsenals and military equipment that were being used by the SPLA in its fight against the Sudanese Government. Any rebel soldiers not already fighting in Sudan quickly gathered around Bonga in a final attempt to secure the fortress. But in spite of their best efforts, they were severely outnumbered and subsequently forced to flee the area.

The other three camps, Dimma, Itang, and Pugnido, having initiated their evacuations days earlier, began the process in an orderly fashion. But because of their vast numbers, the boys were separated into large groups or zones and moved according to the days and times as instructed by their elders. This was done not only to maintain control of the large numbers of boys as they fled the camps, but also to guard against enemy attacks aimed at wiping out the entire population of the unaccompanied minors.

The boys gathered together what meager belongings they had acquired while living in Pugnido, such as pots, pans, plastic jugs, and leftover grain rations, and then waited for their zones to be called to leave. The first groups walked in an unhurried manner, forming long lines that stretched for miles and miles. Their stick-like bodies filled the horizon like tiny ants as they walked toward the main body of the Gilo River. All those fleeing the camps would have to cross the deadly waters in order to reach Sudanese soil. For many, it would prove to be an impossible task. The first group of boys was able to fashion long ropes from area bushes and trees. After securely fastening one end of the rope to a tree or similar anchor, one of the older boys swam across the river with the opposite end of the rope, anchoring it in the same fashion. In this manner, those unable to swim could slowly pull themselves across the river. However, the currents of the Gilo were so strong that many of the younger children were unable to hold on and were subsequently swept away by the swift waters. And so the mass evacuation went.

Meanwhile back in Pugnido, those boys still waiting to be evacuated passed their time by visiting friends and playing games such as dominoes. Dominoes was a favorite game among the boys, one in which they were all quite skilled. And even though they did not have the luxury of store-bought dominoes, they were able to make their own using wood from nearby trees. They did so by carving wood into small rectangular pieces and etching them with small dots by using a crude wood-burning tool made from metal wires heated in a fire.

It was during a more-challenging game of dominoes that some of the boys were caught by surprise as Ethiopian rebels stormed their camp. Following the

SPLA'S defeat in Bonga, the Ethiopian rebels were on a mission to destroy all remaining SPLA soldiers, including anyone suspected of being future soldiers of the SPLA. The rebels began shooting randomly at the boys, forcing them to run from the camp or die sitting on the ground. Without the protection of the SPLA, who were either fighting in Sudan or previously dispatched to Bonga, the unaccompanied minors were left defenseless. Shifting into their ever-familiar mode of survival, the boys did what was now natural instinct: They ran as fast as their feet would carry them.

Those living in Dimma and Itang were faced with similar situations, as they ran from their camps under a cloud of enemy gunfire. They too had to cross portions of the deadly Gilo, and with the rainy season well under way, they knew the swift floodwaters were sure to make it a difficult task. But with the sound of enemy gunfire ringing in their ears, and the rising number of bodies falling around them, the boys quickly scrambled down the muddy banks of the Gilo.

Unaccompanied minors,
having fled Ethiopia,
receive medical treatment
at Nasir

UNHCR/J. Ghedini/ 2004

UNHCR/J. Ghedini/2004

Unaccompanied minor boys

Unaccompanied minor cooking near Nasir

UNHCR/J. Ghedini/2004

When you pass through the waters,
I will be with you...
Isaiah 43:2

The Gilo Exodus
by Isaac Tieng

THE RIVER GILO:
THE WATERS OF DEATH
AND DELIVERANCE

The crossing of the Gilo River would prove to be one of the most memo-rable and horrifying experiences of the Lost Boys' entire journey. Many would die in the deadly waters. Those fleeing Pugnido crossed over the main body of the river, while those fleeing one of the other camps crossed its many tributaries. Regardless of their locations, the stories were all the same.

In the rainy season, the Gilo reaches peak levels in the month of May, when its swollen waters form deep muddy swamps on both sides of its banks, stretch-ing from Pugnido across to Sudan. It was during this season, in May, 1991, that the Lost Boys were forced to cross the Gilo. The deep and turbulent waters awaited them, as rebel soldiers chased them across the muddy banks. Many of the boys dropped what little possessions they carried with them, while struggling through the knee-deep mud. Unable to retrieve their possessions, or simply too tired and frightened to try, the boys left them behind as they quickly moved toward the water. Standing on the banks of the mighty river, the frightened chil-dren were forced to make a life or death decision, given only precious moments to do so. For many, it would be the last decision they would ever make.

If the boys lingered, choosing to stay on the muddy banks as long as possi-ble, the rebel soldiers would surely shoot and kill them. However, if they chose to cross the river, they risked drowning in its swift currents. For those unable to swim, it was a terrifying dilemma. One of the boys told me of an incident in which he saw a boy holding another youth hostage at gunpoint. Distraught at his inability to swim, he had demanded to be carried across the river. Upon reaching the other side, he began to cry uncontrollably, asking the young boy's forgiveness and saying that he had never intended to harm him. But this was

64

only a minor incident, in comparison to the other dangers that awaited the young children.

The waters of the Gilo are host to a variety of spectacular African wildlife such as beautiful birds, exotic fishes, massive hippos, and dangerous crocodiles. All are amazing sights to behold, as they move gracefully in their natural habitats. But looks can often be deceiving, as many of these animals are extremely dangerous when provoked. And as the boys made their way across the murky waters, the vicious and hungry crocodiles lurked beneath its surface, waiting to devour them at random.

The giant hippos, also easily provoked when disturbed, soon joined in the assault, lashing violently at the young intruders. Surrounded by danger, the boys moved frantically across the Gilo, as its water quickly changed to a deep shade of red. Those who survived the blood bath estimate that several thousand Lost Boys died in the Gilo River that day. For those who lived to tell about it, it remains a never-ending nightmare.

JOSEPH GATKUOTH JIECH

NUER REGION

Joseph jumped into the water, swimming frantically across the river. He watched in horror as those around him were killed. The air was thick with their haunting screams, screams that would never be forgotten by those who heard them. They were the cries for help by those unable to swim as they were swept away by the river's swift current, the screams of children as the enemy gunfire reached its target, or the chilling screams of young children being attacked by hippos or caught in a feeding frenzy among vicious crocodiles. The water quickly turned a deep shade of red from their blood.

"The older children (ages 8 to 16) were generally the better swimmers, and they began to carry the younger ones on their backs or take them by the arms and pull them through the water. But there were too many who needed help and not enough of us to help them," recalls Joseph. "We could only watch as they were carried away or disappeared below the water's surface. I was swimming across the water when I heard a young boy beside me screaming for help. It was a really bad scream and I knew something terrible had happened to him. Another boy reached him first and grabbed him by the arm to help him. But when he pulled on his body, it rose to the top of the water and we could see that his bottom half was missing. He was only half a person and yet he continued to scream." Joseph says it was the bite of a hippo that had cut the boy in half.

Most of us envision the lazy, seemingly harmless creatures of children's storybooks when thinking of hippos, dancing gaily in their polka-dot skirts and wearing cute straw hats with flowers stuck inside them. But in reality, they are considered to be some of the most dangerous animals in Africa, killing more people than any other animal including the notoriously vicious crocodile.

Hippos are particularly aggressive when disturbed, as was certainly the case as the frightened young children clambered through the water.

Joseph, who was probably no more than twelve or fourteen years of age at the time, was completely traumatized by what he had witnessed. "I was screaming and crying, and I began to swim as hard as I could in order to reach the other side," he says. "But when I screamed, the water began to fill my mouth, making me cough and choke. I thought I was going to die. All I wanted to do was reach the other side. When I got there I crawled up on the bank still screaming and crying. It was really, really bad. I will never forget that day; even now I still have bad dreams from that day."

The life of a refugee on the run was a role unfamiliar to Joseph. In Sudan before the war reached his village, he had lived in the village of Koch and had been an up-and-coming young hunter as a child, often bringing a feast of wild animals to his family's table.

In those days, Joseph remembers spending fun-filled days with his cousin and best friend Johnson Kueth. They lived next to each other in the village and often worked side by side in their fathers' fields. They usually worked hard at their chores, but never so hard as to prevent them from seeking a new adventure or from getting into a little mischief.

It was such a day while working in their fathers' fields that the two boys spotted a golden opportunity to prove their manhood to their fathers. Of course, they were probably no more than eight years old at the time, but in their minds they were brave warriors and were just about to prove it.

In a nearby field, they spied a baby gazelle, lying in a hole in the ground as it slept. Signaling to one another in their tribal sign language the boys formed their plan of attack. And although they had no bows and arrows or spears, there was no time to worry with details, as the time for attack was now or never.

They ran to the baby gazelle with Johnson grabbing its legs while Joseph grabbed its neck. The gazelle, no larger than an average adult goat, was taken completely by surprise. This did not prevent a struggle, however, as the young gazelle began kicking and butting, tearing at the flesh of its captors in an attempt to fight for its life. After a short time, the boys began to realize that they had no means of securing the wild animal, but they would not be deterred. Johnson quickly sat on top of the gazelle while holding its head, as Joseph stripped nearby bushes, making a rope to tie its legs. Having completed the task, the boys began the 20-minute walk back to their village. After approximately ten minutes—which seemed like years—the boys saw a welcome sight indeed. It was the familiar face of Johnson's father.

Not believing his own eyes, Johnson's father ran to help the courageous and battered young boys, and together they made the long walk home. A big celebration was held at their houses that night, as their families feasted on the young hunters' catch. Later they gathered around the fire, listening to their courageous stories of how they captured the fierce gazelle, stories that became more daring each time they were told. The boys would bear the scars from that adventure for the remainder of their lives, and they would serve as permanent reminders of the day they captured a baby gazelle with their bare hands. But more importantly, those scars would forever remind them of the day they captured the pride of their fathers.

Courageous acts such as this one caused Joseph's father to make an important decision regarding his young son. The elders of the tribe had become very concerned about the civil war in their country and the loss of life among their people. They worried that the customs and traditions of their ancestors would soon be snuffed out, along with the men and young boys of their tribes.

One such custom was the rite of passage, a ceremony generally performed when a young man is between the ages of sixteen and eighteen years old. During this ritual, he is given a particular marking which declares him of the age to marry and also allows him entry into the tribal roles afforded to the men and elders of the tribe. The ritual was called "Gaar."

Joseph's father decided that his son must receive the marking even though he was no more than nine years of age at the time. The decision was made in an effort to preserve the customs of their people.

Gaar is a series of six straight lines that are carved across the foreheads of young Nuer men. Many tribes of Africa have similar markings, but they often vary in an effort to distinguish one tribe from another. If you bear the mark of Gaar on your forehead, it is proof to all those who behold you that you are indeed very strong. It is a mark that young Nuer men must bear in order to earn the title of "man." A special person called the "Gur" is trained in the procedure and is the only person qualified to perform such a ceremony. If there is not a Gur residing in the village of the young man that requires him, then one must be sent from a neighboring village.

This person holds the respect and training similar to that of a Moil in the Jewish faith, the person who performs the ceremony of circumcision. Although this ceremony has nothing to do with circumcision, it also requires precision and special training. The preparations leading up to the event of the Gaar ceremony are also a grand production like that of a full-scale Bar Mitzvah.

The day before the ceremony was to be held, the women began preparing special foods to be served on the momentous occasion. This was a laborious and time-consuming task, as everyone in the village was to be invited. In addition to the various foods served, a special wine was prepared from grains for the enjoyment of the elders. It was a grand celebration lasting into the wee hours of the night. The elders also performed a special tribal dance during this event, in which they beat themselves repeatedly across their backs with the leaves of sorghum plants, while dancing round the fire to the rhythm of the drums.

A cow was also sacrificed in honor of the occasion and its meat served as part of the celebration meal. This was a rare treat for the villagers, because the cow was a much revered animal and rarely eaten unless in conjunction with a special occasion or sacrificial ceremony.

"Even in the dry season when there was little food and we were very hungry, we would not eat the meat of a cow," says Joseph. "If we became too hungry, we bled the cow in order to maintain our strength. We did this by tying a rope tightly around the cow's neck to increase the blood flow. When the rope was released we made a hole in its protruding vein." The blood that poured from the opening in the vein was captured inside a gourd or clay bowl, and then boiled making a broth to be used in soups. When gathering a sufficient supply of blood, the rope was fastened once again around the neck of the cow in order to stop the bleeding and prevent it from becoming too weak. "The blood of the cow made us very strong," said Joseph.

Although the meat of the cow was eaten only on special occasions, the villagers used various other by-products on a daily basis. The dung was often burned, creating a smoky haze said to repel the disease-carrying flies and mosquitoes which swarmed the village. The remaining ash was rubbed on the bodies of the villagers creating a whitish gray sheen that they considered a decoration for their bodies. It was also used in their hair to control bugs (most likely lice), and it was even used as toothpaste to clean their teeth. "It makes the teeth very white and beautiful to behold," Joseph proclaims with a broad smile. (I must agree that most Sudanese have extremely white teeth, but I prefer Crest just the same, thank you.) The urine from the cow was used for washing their hands and also in various dishes routinely eaten by the villagers. The milk was used for drinking and in making cheese. The hide of the cow was used for clothing and other items such as rugs, blankets, drums, etc. But on this particular day, the cow was used as a sacrifice in Joseph's honor.

The members of the tribe watched anxiously as one of the elders pierced the heart of the cow with his spear, and then gathered around it to witness its final fall before dying. It was not the actual killing of the cow that had gained their undivided attention but rather the fall itself that intrigued them.

The direction in which the cow fell was extremely significant, as it determined whether or not God would choose to bless Joseph's passage into manhood. If the cow fell on its right side, it was a bad omen and the family must ask God why He had made this decision. But if the cow fell on its left side, it meant that God had chosen to give His blessing to Joseph. The villagers crowded around the cow watching closely as it stumbled several times before coming to a complete stop. And then, while taking its last breath of life, the cow fell to the ground landing on its left side, declaring Joseph to be blessed by God.

After closely shaving his head with an instrument similar to a large razor from the early days of the American west, Joseph was made to lie on his back on the ground. His head was situated between two holes, which had been dug in the ground beneath him, serving as reservoirs to catch the blood when it spilled from his forehead. The Gur then began the painful process of the Gaar ritual, permanently etching vertical lines across Joseph's forehead. Sometimes these lines are cut so deep that they reach the underlying bone. In fact, human remains have been found in this region revealing the markings of Gaar deeply etched in skulls.

"I was not frightened, and I was very proud that I did not cry even though it hurt very badly. I had nothing for pain," he says defiantly. "We could not be made to drink the wine because then we might go crazy or something like that and bleed to death!" (Drinking was reserved only for those over forty years of age and the rites of passage were no exception.)

Some people did cry during the ritual, according to Joseph. Some even squirmed and wiggled their bodies in pain. And although crying was permitted, according to Joseph, movement during the procedure could result in jagged lines across your forehead instead of the desired straight and even ones. "This was not a good thing," says Joseph, "because if your lines became crooked, you were permanently marked as a coward."

This proved to be unbearable for some of the mothers whose sons received the marking of a coward on their foreheads. These mothers were said to have hanged themselves in shame. But Joseph's lines were perfectly straight, and his mother was very proud.

Joseph had been very brave during the rites of Gaar, but there would be no lavish meals or partying for him. Joseph was taken instead to the hut of his Grandmother where he lay outside until the bleeding subsided. Someone was stationed beside him during this time with a fan made out of leaves to prevent the flies from landing on his wounds. It took several days for the bleeding to stop. When it did, Joseph was taken inside the hut and placed in a special room made just for him for his recovery. One of the older women remained with him at all times watching over him and making sure he did not turn his head sideways. "If I turned my head sideways, she would slap me really hard," Joseph remembers. "Turning your head could cause a lot of bleeding and you could die from this."

Walls were erected from mud to give him privacy, but he was allowed to move only when he needed to go to the bathroom. He was allowed only soft foods during this time to prevent excessive chewing that may cause bleeding. Recovering from Gaar could take up to two months, during which time Joseph was required to stay in his Grandmother's hut in the care of the women of his family. He was also kept away from his prized cattle during this time, for fear he would catch some sort of disease from them while recovering.

When Joseph finally emerged from his hut having fully recovered from Gaar, he made a trip down to the river to bathe. At this time, the men of the family—his father, brothers, grandfathers, and uncles—gave Joseph special tokens in honor of his passage into manhood. They each give him a bracelet or a necklace that they had made from bone, or ones that they had received in trade with the "Jalabni," the Arab traders who traveled through the villages on horseback. Each man in his family also gave him a spear to be used in hunting wild animals and in protecting the village. "When the British came, they built bridges over some of the rivers so that they could travel over them in their trucks. We had no use for such things, so we removed the nails and metal pieces from the bridges and we made spears with them."

Joseph was now considered a man in his tribe and was fully equipped for the many future hunting expeditions he would take part in. But the first such expedition he must undertake alone, with no outside help. It was to be one of the most important of his hunting expeditions, one that could possibly affect him for the rest of his life. Joseph was about to embark on the daring and exhilarating hunt for a woman!

"This must be done immediately," he recalls. "There must be no waiting." Apparently Joseph had been scouting out the territory ahead of time, because he made his choice quickly. Of course, this was only the beginning stage of courtship and no promises or demands for marriage were made. This was just a way of staking his claim on a girl whom he wanted to get to know a little better. Joseph becomes quite embarrassed when asked about this, and he absolutely refused to give me any information regarding his selection of a woman on that day.

Having picked his woman and having carried the catch of many animals under his belt, Joseph had been regarded highly as an accomplished hunter in the village of Koch. But as he swam across the Gilo River, fleeing enemy soldiers and wild animals that lurked beneath the waters, Joseph realized that his life had taken a horrifying twist—because the accomplished hunter had now become the hunted.

The Nightmare Returns
by John Yok

SUDAN:
THE NIGHTMARE
RETURNS

Following their flight from Ethiopia and the deadly crossing of the Gilo River, the Lost Boys traveling from Pugnido, in numbers of nearly 16,000 by some counts, journeyed to Pochala (Pa-cho-la), just inside the Sudanese border. Those traveling from Dimma settled in an area known as Pakok, while the majority of those fleeing from Itang traveled to Nasir. Food supplies were extremely low or nonexistent in the makeshift camps, where starvation had already begun to take its toll. Some of the boys began disappearing into the bush shortly after their arrival in an attempt to find their families, or in a desperate search for food. Others joined the ranks of the SPLA, in an effort to bring peace to their homeland. However, the majority of the boys living in Pochala, our primary focus for now, remained there due to their weakened conditions, or for fear of leaving the relative safety of the camp. Most viewed attempts at locating their families as futile at this point, assuming their villages to be destroyed and their friends and families dead, captured, or displaced. In the majority of cases, those assumptions were valid.

Those remaining in Pochala were assisted primarily by the SPLA and the International Committee of the Red Cross (ICRC). According to ICRC reports, there were approximately 10,000 unaccompanied male minors living within the camp in the most deplorable of conditions. Food and water were scarce, and any attempts at delivering fresh supplies, allowable only by air, were often hampered due to poor weather conditions or enemy activity in the area. When much needed supplies finally did arrive, they were often in insufficient quantities to feed the thousands of refugees living in the camp. On average, each boy received one cup of lentils, one cup of wheat, and when available, one cup of oil to last them for a period of fifteen days.

According to various surveys taken at the camps in Pakok, Pochala, and Nasir in 1991, up to 66% of the unaccompanied minor population suffered from moderate malnutrition. One of the boys named Peter Kok told me a story in which he and a friend were sitting on the ground talking. Suddenly his friend began to look sleepy, and shortly thereafter his friend closed his eyes and fell to the ground, landing on his side. Peter poked his friend in an attempt to arouse him, but his friend was unresponsive. Peter then noticed a small trickle of blood coming from his friend's nose and began to poke him more vigorously, to no avail. Much to his horror, Peter soon realized that his friend, who was only ten or twelve years of age at the time, had died as they were talking. "We were so hungry," Peter sighs, "but there was not enough food and there was nothing we could do about it."

Further north, on the Sobat River Basin in Nasir, professional photographer Wendy Stone was on assignment for UNICEF, photographing the relief work being done by a UNICEF medical team who were assessing the medical needs of the Sudanese children. Nasir was to be her final destination in Sudan, and upon finishing her work there Ms. Stone began making her final preparations for the return flight home to Kenya. Ms. Stone's plans hit a snag, however, as the rainy season began and torrential rains suddenly poured from the sky. Originally scheduled to spend only a few days in Nasir, Ms. Stone now found herself stranded in the desolate bush of Nasir. "Nasir was not a place where you wanted to stay," she says. "The conditions which included rain, mosquitoes, and mud up to our ankles were difficult to cope with."

In the midst of such difficult conditions, relief workers in Nasir received an alarming radio dispatch informing them that more than 1,000 children, fleeing on foot from the Itang refugee camp in Ethiopia, were headed in their direction. Just after waking the next day, Ms. Stone looked off into the horizon and saw streams of thousands of children walking toward her. "They looked like little specks that stretched for miles and miles," she said. "They had been walking for approximately ten days with no food and little water. And they seemed to just be walking—walking home." The boys were dazed and in shock, starving and completely exhausted, their legs and feet covered with cuts and sores. "It was one of the most emotional experiences of my life." Ms. Stone also remembered that several older men traveling with the boys seemed to be in charge of directing the youths. When they reached Nasir, the older men commanded the boys to stop walking and in doing so, the boys immediately fell to the ground. "There was no talking amongst them," recounted Ms. Stone. "The only sound heard was that of thousands of small bodies as they fell to the ground. They collapsed in small heaps, one piled on top of the other. And then in a matter of seconds they were all asleep, as total exhaustion swept over them."

The next day, the small medical team began moving through the crowd of young children, made up of both girls and boys, evaluating and assessing their condition. Like those in Pochala, they were also in desperate need of food and medical attention. But due to the heavy rains and muddy conditions on the ground, relief planes were unable to land. Food rations among the relief workers began to dwindle as well, leaving workers without substantial food for several days. "We had only a few crackers, some peanut butter, and canned tuna to share amongst ourselves," remembered Ms. Stone, "but in view of the tremendous suffering of these young boys, our own hunger was not important."

Several days later, to the relief of all those in Nasir, UN planes began flying overhead dropping food to the boys and workers below. It would be three more days, however, before UN planes carrying doctors, medical supplies, and additional food were able to land. Not knowing the complete story of the Lost Boys at that time, or the magnitude of their plight, Ms. Stone, who had subsequently run out of film, left Nasir assuming that the boys would be safe and well cared for by UN and UNICEF staff; both to whom she gives credit for their tireless efforts in this war. But with GOS forces hot on their trail, the boys were not able to stay long. Commanded by their elders, they were forced to leave Nasir, continuing on a journey that some say led them straight to the holding camps for the future soldiers of the SPLA.

In the days and months that lay ahead, there would be much more than mere miles to separate the Lost Boys in Nasir from those in Pochala. Because in August of 1991, three months after their flight from Ethiopia, Nuer tribesman Riek Machar, along with tribesmen Gordon Kong Chol and Lam Akol, split from Garang forming their own faction of the SPLA known as the SPLA-Nasir, later becoming known as the Southern Sudan Independence Movement/Army or SSIM/A. Some say the split was the result of a power struggle between Riek Machar and John Garang. But Machar cited human rights violations as the primary reason for the split, claiming that Garang used underage children within his ranks of the SPLA. This charge later boomeranged, however, coming right back to Machar, who was also cited for the same violation. SPLA spokesperson Stephen Wondu, stationed in Washington D.C., explained the controversy surrounding underage soldiers in this way. "When someone is shooting your mother and father in front of you and burning down everything around you, you don't have time to stop and think. You pick up a gun and you fight!"

Other reasons listed by Machar for the split with Garang were his clear lack of objectives regarding the future of the South and also his Marxist dictator-like style. But regardless of the real issues behind their split, the GOS quickly used the split to its advantage, giving credence to the propaganda that the civil war of Sudan was a battle among tribes and not between the North and South. In making these claims, it appears that the GOS hoped to publicly relinquish itself from the atrocities occurring in the South under its command. And in a further effort to lend credibility to this absurd notion of tribal conflicts, the GOS reportedly formed an alliance with Riek Machar and his compatriots, supplying them with guns and munitions to be used in their fight against Garang and those aligned with him. However, Professor David Chand, a former top commander and spokesperson for the SPLA-Nasir, tells me that those allegations are false and instigated by Garang for the sole purpose of gaining support among Southerners in the battle against Machar.

As the struggle for power intensified between the two rebel militias, members of Riek Machar's faction rose up against Garang's forces, launching a full-scale attack against Garang's hometown district of Bor, resulting in a massacre unlike any other previously recorded in SPLA history. In retaliation, members of Garang's faction launched a brutal attack against those living in the birth-place of Riek Machar. Caught in the crossfire of the dueling rebel militias were the thousands of innocent Sudanese Southerners who lay dead as a result, in numbers that some say reached higher than any previous attacks launched by GOS forces. Both rebel leaders later denied having authorized the attacks, claiming that they had been the actions of a few rogue soldiers.

By all outward appearances, the civil war of Sudan had indeed become one among tribes—the Nuer pitted against the Dinka. But in talking to the Lost Boys and SPLA spokespeople, nothing could be further from the truth. Each claims that the split was due primarily to the geographical locations to which the boys fled from Ethiopia, and insist emphatically that it never had anything to do with tribal conflicts between the two. They explain that the boys residing in Pochala and Pakok, under the leadership of Garang, had fled primarily from the Pugnido and Dimma camps, with Pugnido having been heavily populated by Dinkas. Those living in Nasir, now under the leadership of Machar, had fled primarily from the Itang camp, heavily populated by the Nuer. Therefore, the split within the SPLA was more geographical in nature than anything else and had nothing to do with a separation of tribes between the Nuer and the Dinka. In fact, the majority of the Nuer boys living in Pochala remained with Garang, choosing to fight alongside him in his faction of the SPLA. But as the struggle for power continued between the two rebel leaders, the South began losing ground, relinquishing long-held territories to GOS forces who were only too happy to claim them as their own.

Meanwhile, Ethiopian rebels, still aligned with the GOS, continued their assaults against the Lost Boys and the accompanying SPLA forces by directing guided missiles toward their camps in Pochala from nearby Ethiopian borders. GOS Anatov fighter jets reinforced these assaults by dropping bombs on the young children from Sudanese airspace. In an attempt to protect themselves, the children dug foxholes outside their tukuls using their bare hands or the branches from nearby trees. Fortunately, the ground was soft in the aftermath of the rainy season and was a welcome reprieve for the malnourished and weakened young boys.

As land and air assaults against the boys intensified, those in Pochala were forced to flee their makeshift huts and travel under the cover of night to join the others in Pakok (pronounced paa-cook). Those unable to withstand the journey, due to illness or the sheer lack of strength, were left behind under the care and supervision of a few brave teachers and elders who had graciously volunteered to stay and care for them. Shortly after the majority of the boys had departed, GOS forces seized Pochala killing or capturing all those too weak to flee. "Many people lost their lives that day," said one boy. Those who managed to escape quickly made their way to Pakok, announcing the fall of Pochala and warning the others of eminent attacks by GOS forces.

After resting for only one night in Pakok, the boys hastily made their way south to Boma, where they remained only a short time before embarking on a particularly grueling trek across the Kathangor desert. "We did not wish to cross the desert," said one boy. "We had no food or water, and we knew without a doubt that we would surely die. But the elders forced us to continue by the use of physical punishments and also with the promise that we would receive water when reaching the Koragarap River." With the rainy season having just come to an end, it was assumed that the river would be filled with water. But upon reaching the river—or what was left of it—all hope was dashed as the boys found only muddy puddles to greet them. Desperate for water by this time due to the arduous journey across the hot desert sands, many of the boys began vigorously eating the mud, in a futile attempt to quench their overpowering thirst. Others with only precious little strength to sustain them began frantically digging in the muddy soil in search of roots from Amoyoak plants, which have the ability to separate mud from water, according to the boys. When finding the much sought after roots, they began to scoop as much mud as possible into all available containers and then buried the roots deep beneath the muddy mixture. "After some time," said the boys, "the mud settled to the bottom of the container and water floated to the surface." But it was not murky water, as one would expect. Instead it was crystal clear due to the cleansing property of roots.

Having temporarily quenched their thirst, the boys continued on their journey to the town of Magus (pronounced Maa-goose). Bringing up the rear, in the last zone of boys to make their way across the desert, was the sick, injured, and youngest of the groups. The perilous trek had been extremely hard on this particular group of boys, leaving them at considerable risk for death. When nearing the town of Magus (also known as Magoth), having deteriorated to the point at which they could barely walk or stand, the boys had begun to lose all hopes for survival. But while looking off into the distance, they saw what appeared to be a mirage. Surely their minds were playing tricks on them! But the low rumbling sounds of the trucks gave credence to their visions, proving that they were not hallucinating. Instead the boys were witnessing an approaching convoy of ICRC vehicles sent to rescue and carry them to the town of Magus. When they reached Magus, the boys received much needed food and water before being transported to Kapoeta (pronounced Kay-po-eh-tah), where they would receive medical attention as well.

Those traveling by foot reached the desolate bush of Magus sometime later, where much to their surprise they were greeted by a lone ICRC aid worker. Adding to their disbelief was the fact that the aid worker was a woman. "We couldn't believe our eyes," declared the boys. "This woman had prepared a camp for us in that place, in the middle of nowhere, and had remained in the bush all night by herself, giving no thought for her own safety. She also gave us food and water when we arrived, which made us very happy because we were really hungry at this time."

As the long procession of boys began to file into the camp, the woman began to sob uncontrollably at the sight of them. When she saw the elders, she began to shout at them. "How can you force these young boys to continue walking in their condition?" she demanded. "What is wrong with you? Can't you see they're just children?"

The stay in Magus was somewhat longer than that in Pakok and Boma, lasting approximately a week or so. But soon the same old scenario began to repeat itself with GOS assaults resuming, forcing the boys to flee at nightfall once again to the town of Kapoeta, approximately fifty miles to the south. The boys traveled without the use of flashlights, which were unavailable, or torches that would have surely alerted the GOS. "Our elders were very familiar with the paths and roadways that we traveled, because they had traveled on them many times before the war and since," explained the boys.

But when traveling in those areas that were unfamiliar, the elders solicited assistance from individuals among the indigenous tribes, those who would not betray their lives. And when all else failed, they simply cast their eyes to the sky, and like their ancestors before them, they used the moon and stars to guide them. Looking back, the boys marvel at the fact that, even though they believed the machines in outer space (satellites) were tracking their every move, they were still able as small children to elude GOS soldiers, sometimes missing their intended date with death by mere minutes or hours. The Lost Boys attribute their good fortune solely to God, saying that He watched over them every step of the way.

Starving and barely able to walk, the boys journeyed on, their bodies a living canvas of the suffering and pain they'd endured. Each bore deep cuts on their bodies from the thick and razor-sharp thorns of the African bush, and most walked in pools of blood due to the battered conditions of their unprotected feet. Many displayed the open wounds of the Guinea worm, a parasite that exits the body of its carrier by boring gaping holes through its flesh. While countless other Lost Boys, riddled by gunfire and shrapnel, gave living testament to the brutal attacks launched against them, as evidenced by the deep scars on their bodies and the bullets lodged deep within their flesh and bones.

Adding to their treacherous walk were encounters with unfriendly tribesmen of the time, such as the fierce Toposa warriors. When crossing Toposa land, the ruthless tribesmen were said to have accosted many of the Lost Boys, stealing what few possessions they had managed to hold on to, leaving nothing unscathed. Even the tattered clothing they wore on their backs was taken, leaving them completely exposed to the harsh elements and disease-carrying mosquitoes that attacked them day and night. Those refusing to relinquish their belongings were reportedly shot and killed.

The boys remained in Kapoeta for approximately one to four weeks (depending on their zone's arrival time) before GOS forces were able to pinpoint their location. Once again they were forced to flee, but this time, in addition to the constant threat of GOS militia, was the added danger of the Toposa tribesmen. Although the boys had achieved a somewhat peaceful relationship with the Toposa by this time, Toposa spies routinely visited their camp in an effort to gather information about them and the SPLA. With this in mind, the boys were warned by their elders not to discuss their plans of departure with any of the Toposa. "Had the Toposa learned of our plans," says one boy, "they would have made big trouble for us."

As daylight transcended into darkness, the long caravan of boys slipped silently into the night, their black bodies camouflaged against the dark sky, rendering them invisible to the eyes of evil that watched their every move. Walking some 75 miles toward the southeast the boys reached the town of Narus, where they remained for approximately six months until learning of the fall of Kapoeta. Soon thereafter, they found themselves surrounded by GOS forces. And under a barrage of heavy gunfire, both by land and air, the boys ran for their lives to the town of Lokichokio (called Loki or "low-key" for short), just inside the country of Kenya on the southeastern border of Sudan.

Assisted by the ICRC, the boys set up camp in Loki with no assurance of how long they would remain there. Once again, using sticks and branches from nearby trees they constructed makeshift tukuls, covering them with plastic tarps provided by the UNHCR. And although the boys were afforded a reprieve from GOS forces, since any attacks against the Lost Boys while on Kenyan soil would have ignited a war between Sudan and Kenya, their lives continued to be difficult. There were at least 10,000 Lost Boys living in the camp at that time, in addition to the numerous displaced Sudanese families who traveled with them. And although meager food rations were distributed regularly among the refugees, water was still in short supply, as there was only one well located within the camp. The ICRC tried to compensate for the shortage of water by bringing in large tankers on a daily basis. But since the arrival times of those tankers was very unpredictable, the boys were often required to stand in line from before sunrise to after sunset to ensure that they received water. Many days, the tankers ran out before the long lines ended and, after waiting all day in the hot sun, the Lost Boys were turned away empty-handed. "On those days, we went directly to the well where we were often made to wait in line all night before receiving any water," says John Kuai. "We received one jar can (a large oil drum similar to a gasoline container) of drinking water," says John. I commented that this seemed like an ample amount of water, to which John laughingly replied, "The water we received was not only for our own use, but for that of our entire group, approximately 50 people." The next day, the process would be repeated once again.

The boys remained in Loki for approximately three months before being offered asylum by the Kenyan government and relocated to the Kakuma Refugee Camp in northwestern Kenya. By this time, it was the summer of 1992, and the boys had been walking, running, and hiding in the dangerous and desolate bush of Sudan for over a year since their mass exodus from Ethiopia. Most had walked in excess of 1,000 miles since fleeing their villages in Southern Sudan. And although the Lost Boys had come from many different regions and villages, speaking numerous dialects and practicing varying customs, they now shared one thing in common: Each boy was truly a miracle.

STEPHEN MAJAK DENG

NUER REGION

Shortly after meeting him, you know that Stephen Deng is one of those people you want to take under your wings where you can love and care for him and hopefully, in some way, make his life a better one. Like most young people, he is strong-willed and stubborn at times. But beneath that strong exterior lies a sweet and gentle spirit, in spite of the many hardships and terrors he's endured.

Like many others, Stephen spent much of his early days running from GOS soldiers. When he finally reached Ethiopia, he had hoped he could remain there safely, until the war ended in his own country. Unfortunately that was not to be, as once again Stephen found himself being chased by enemy soldiers, their deadly bullets singing all too familiar songs of death as they flew past his ears. Only this time he was running from the bullets of Ethiopian rebels, who had aligned themselves with the GOS in an attempt to overthrow the Ethiopian government. As civil war erupted in Ethiopia, what had once been a safe haven for Stephen and other Lost Boys had now become a killing field, littered with the bodies of those innocent men, women, and children who had come to Ethiopia in search of refuge. They knew only that they must run, and no matter where their final destination would be, they must reach it quickly. Most ran in the same direction as those who had previously fled the camp, retracing the heavily trodden path that would lead them ultimately back into Sudan—straight into the hands of the GOS.

Unlike many of the Lost Boys, who had years earlier escaped the GOS militia as they stormed their villages, Stephen had been captured and taken prisoner by them. He had witnessed the enemy firsthand, and the thought of being captured by the GOS once again caused him to tremble with fear.

He remembers that day clearly, as if it were only yesterday. Government soldiers came to his village in the middle of the night while Stephen, as was customary, lay sleeping with his brother and father in a straw tukul housing the men of the family. His mother and sister slept nearby, in a separate tukul on the comfort of a straw mat reserved only for the women.

Stephen, about five or six years old at the time, remembers waking to the thunderous sound of soldiers as they stormed through his village. There was no warning! They came like thieves in the night with guns and machetes, killing everyone in sight and then stealing the livestock and food. Many of the women and young girls were taken as slaves. The crops, not yet harvested, were torched and burned to the ground, along with the homes of the villagers and all the possessions within them.

Stephen became separated from his family in the darkness and mayhem, but somehow managed to escape into the bush unharmed. He remained there, hidden for most of the night, along with nine other young children. Each waited silently in the tall grass, praying they would be safe from the enemy. But the soldiers left no stone unturned that night. After destroying the village, they began marching through the bush looking for all survivors who might be hiding there.

Soon they stumbled upon ten young children, huddled together tightly. Among them was Stephen. After assembling the children together in a small group, the soldiers tied their wrists behind their backs and threw them into the open end of a large supply truck. As dawn made its way across the landscape, the children were driven to a field where a lone straw hut stood ominously in the distance. One by one, the soldiers escorted the children to the hut. "It was very far away," Stephen recalls. "We had to walk maybe a mile to reach it." Those who remained behind waited anxiously for the others to return, hoping to receive some sort of indication as to what they could expect when their turn came. However, what the young children didn't realize at the time was that the others who left before them would never return.

As Stephen recalls, he was the fifth or sixth child to be taken away. "I walked inside the hut," he says, "and noticed immediately that none of the others who went before me remained." Stephen then feared that perhaps the soldier standing in front of him had thrown them into the ground (meaning a mass grave). "He didn't wish to obtain any information from me," Stephen remembers. "He asked me only one question: 'Are you a Christian?' I said, 'Yes.'"

At that point, the soldier told Stephen to kneel before him on the ground. "But as I knelt there, something shiny caught my eye. I turned my head to see what it was just as the soldier attempted to cut my throat." This caused the soldier to miss his mark and cut through Stephen's ear instead, almost cutting it off. Blood went everywhere. "The pain was very bad. I was no longer inside my body. I was on the outside of myself. Suddenly I had strength that I was not capable of. I ran right through the wall of that straw hut!" Stephen didn't stop running for two days.

Several days later, aid workers from the ICRC spotted Stephen alone, running frantically through the African bush. Still in shock and traumatized by his encounter with the soldier, the aid workers had to chase him down and catch him like a wild animal. After stitching his ear and giving him some food and water, they took Stephen to join a group of boys on their way to Ethiopia. Together they walked to the distant country, knowing little about what to expect when they arrived, but praying they would be safe. At five or six years old, Stephen was on his own and must now learn to fend for himself.

Stephen is unsure why the soldier never came after him that day. However, he still bears the scar from that encounter on his left ear, a daily reminder of God's protection over his life.

Stephen would need that protection many times in the days and years to come, such as when traveling back into Sudan after fleeing from Ethiopia. Enemy soldiers were not the only dangers the young boys faced while walking through the wilds of Africa. They also encountered numerous wild and hungry animals, lurking in the bush.

Following their escape from Pugnido, the Lost Boys traveled in large caravans. The stronger, faster boys generally walked in front, while the younger, weaker ones walked further behind. And then, of course, there were always those scattered few, like Stephen, who walked somewhere in between.

On this particular day, just as daylight and dusk began to trade places, the boys began to slow their pace as another long day was ending. Stephen was traveling in a small group consisting of only three boys, each walking in single file through the bush. Stephen was the last in the line.

The larger group of boys, traveling up ahead, had vanished from sight. Likewise, those traveling behind had also dropped out of sight, leaving Stephen and his friends completely alone in the dangerous wilds of the bush. Stephen assumed that the others had most likely stopped to prepare their camps for the night, and with nightfall quickly approaching they began to search frantically for the group ahead of them. Darkness, like a heavy blanket, began to cover the sky above them, and Stephen and the others quickened their pace, walking a little faster in an effort to catch the group in front of them.

Stephen saw it first and watched as the grass moved in a slow and steady pattern towards them. "The screaming began in my head like a bad dream that you struggle unsuccessfully to wake from," he says. "But before the sound could escape my lips the movement had quickened and the intruder had begun his assault." Stephen watched in horror as the large lion jumped from beneath the cover of the bush, quickly grabbing the first boy in line and dragging him back to the tall grass, laying him aside for later. Then quickly, in a matter of seconds, the lion was back again for the next boy. "It happened so fast that it was a blur," remembers Stephen. "There was no time for screaming." The lion had grabbed both boys by the throats, carrying them like defenseless tattered rag dolls into the bush, as Stephen watched helplessly. He stood rooted to that spot, frozen in time, motionless like a statue for over three hours. Witnessing the death of his two friends, Stephen understandably assumed he would be the lion's final victim.

With this thought, Stephen bolstered the courage needed to make a run for it. The only possessions he had been carrying with him were a small bag filled with his precious few belongings and a crude straw hat that shielded his eyes and face from the relentless African sun. Both were dropped to the ground for fear that they may touch the grass and warn the lion of his presence. And then, with only his life in tow, Stephen ran—something to which he had grown accustomed in his short lifetime. It seemed that he was always running, running, running.

Racing ahead, Stephen caught up to the first group of boys and told them what had happened to his two friends. Thinking he was merely a young boy with an overactive imagination the elders of the tribe (who were no more than sixteen or seventeen years of age) walked back with him the next day, certain they would find his young friends. But all they found that day was the path of a lion, leading into the bush where the remains of his two friends lay.

Stephen believes that God rendered him invisible to the lion that day. And with his right hand held outward in a tightly clinched fist, he declares, "I know this is true... I know this is true because He was holding me right here in the palm of His hand all of the time."

It is reported that 3-5 displaced children in Southern Sudan are eaten weekly by wild animals as they hide in the bush from enemy soldiers. In hearing those reports, one can only pray that God will also hold the remaining children of Southern Sudan tightly in the palm of His right hand.

Makeshift tukuls at Lokichokio

Unaccompanied minors play game of "tok kurou" in Lokichokio

The Classroom
by Isaac Tieng

"Hi, you people! You gave us the word of God and then you left us in the darkness. You know that there are those who are persecuting us because we believe in God.

Oh, America, don't you see us? Hasn't God opened your eyes? If you really know about us, then do your work. See the people who are thinking about you and praying for your power.

Thank you for your reply in advance."

Jacob R. Angok
Lost Boy from Kakuma Refugee Camp

KENYA:
KAKUMA REFUGEE CAMP

In August of 1992, the Kenyan government, in conjunction with the UNHCR, established the Kakuma Refugee Camp in an effort to accommodate the large influx of Sudanese refugees (mostly unaccompanied young boys) who had been granted asylum in that country.

Kakuma, located in the northwestern tip of Kenya in a region known as the Turkana district, rests on a dry and barren stretch of land bordering Sudan, Uganda, and Ethiopia. For the most part, it is useless land, due to the lack of fresh water or fertile soil in which to grow crops or vegetation. The blistering Kenyan sun burns with an intense heat for most of the day in that region, reaching temperatures in the 100-degree range or higher. As a result, the earth beneath its scorching rays has been rendered dusty wasteland, littered with empty riverbeds that once flowed with water, but now lie lifeless—except for the Saturday gatherings of refugees who sing songs of hope and praise from the deep banks of their despair.

Fierce winds howl continuously across the desert sands of Kakuma, creating a thick red haze that chokes all who walk across the barren land. Some of the only creatures that can withstand it are the poisonous snakes, deadly scorpions, and spiders. Many Kenyans refer to the Turkana District as "no-man's land," rightfully so, as it is truly a desolate and forsaken place, filled with the forgotten peoples of Northern Africa.

The local people living in the area surrounding the camp are called the "Turkanas." For the most part, they are a poor and downtrodden people who survive primarily on the small herds of malnourished goats, donkeys, and camels they tend. In the aftermath of continuous cycles of drought and famine, and after receiving little help from their government or the outside world, the Turkanas have become destitute. Many Turkanas, who were once friendly with the refugees of Kakuma, have now become envious of them, resenting the aid offered to the refugees, while they, themselves, continue to suffer and starve on their own land.

In addition to hosting the multitude of Sudanese refugees, the gates of Kakuma were later opened to a host of other refugees fleeing from countries such as Somalia, Ethiopia, Rwanda, Burundi, Uganda, Congo, Eritrea, the Democratic Republic of Congo, and Liberia. As a result, the camp's population now surpasses 80,000, whose requirements exceed by far the available amount of food and water, leading to malnutrition and dehydration in the majority of the camp's population.

Initially, food rations were delivered to group leaders within the camp, who in turn distributed them among the various groups of refugees. But in 1995, distribution centers were built, requiring the refugees to travel to the center nearest them to receive their rations. "This decision," says one Lost Boy, "was the worst decision ever made in Kakuma." Not only did the opening of these distribution centers require the refugees to travel great distances in order to receive their food, it required them to wait in extremely long lines as well.

Even though the distribution centers were placed throughout the camp, in Zones 1 and 2, and later in the newer Phases II and III, they proved grossly inept at meeting the needs of the large masses of people. On many occasions, the boys awoke as early as 3 a.m. to secure their place in line, only to be turned away empty handed as late as 5 p.m. the same day, due to the large numbers of people waiting in line. On days in which they did receive rations, they were faced with yet another problem, that of storage. Although their food rations were meant to last them for 15 to 30 days, depending on the amount they received, the boys had no cabinets or refrigerators in which to store the food, leaving it susceptible to mold and animals, such as rodents. However, the latter were not serious threats, as the amount of food the boys received was not enough to satisfy even the bellies of small rodents. The bigger problem—the Turkanas.

There have been numerous reports of violence between the Turkanas and the refugees including fighting, gunfire, rape, and the looting of food and personal property belonging to the refugees. On occasion, these incidents have resulted in serious injuries or death to refugees. And although the camp's perimeter is regularly patrolled by Kenyan police and UNHCR officials, it seems of little consequence, as the Turkanas continue to sneak into the camp at night, armed with guns, pillaging anything of value they can get their hands on. The boys, when approached by the Turkanas, willingly relinquished their food and belongings, realizing that in doing so, they would remain hungry for many days before receiving additional rations. "What else could we do?" says Lost Boy John Kuai. "If we refused to give them our food, they would have killed us anyway, so we just took our chances with the hunger."

Even after inhabiting the same land for many years, the relationship between the Turkanas and the refugees continues to be an unstable one. Not only are the refugees warned to stay in their tukuls at night, they are also encouraged to remain within the confines of the camp at all times unless traveling in groups. Women are especially vulnerable and are frequently raped while gathering firewood outside the camp perimeter.

The poor and weakened state of the refugees leaves them susceptible to a variety of diseases such as malaria, typhoid, cholera, and hepatitis. If left untreated, they often result in death. John Kuai remembers an outbreak of cholera in the camp around 1995, which he says claimed the lives of over 400 refugees, many of whom were Lost Boys. In an effort to prevent future outbreaks, camp officials instructed the refugees in the basic steps of proper sanitation, such as boiling water before drinking it, as well as proper maintenance of their lavatory facilities.

No indoor plumbing is available to the refugees, but public facilities (essentially large outhouses) have been built in an effort to accommodate their overwhelming sanitation needs. These facilities, for the most part, are simply large holes that have been dug deep into the ground and covered with round cement floors. A small hole is fashioned in the center of the floor complete with mud pedestals on each side, where the refugees must stand or squat in order to relieve themselves. In an effort to ensure privacy, the facilities are covered with thatched roofs and mud walls, but all forms of luxury stop there as the boys must use coarse paper towels or leftover school papers in order to clean themselves. Chemicals supplied by camp officials are used on a regular basis in an effort to disinfect and disintegrate the accumulated waste matter. But when chemicals are no longer effective, the facility is closed and a new one is built in another location.

Initially, the International Rescue Committee established a rudimentary health clinic in Zone 1, which operated for many years inside the confines of a large tent. Eventually, a permanent facility was built using mud bricks, and it continues to serve as the primary hospital in Kakuma. In addition to the main hospital, smaller clinics operate in Zones 2, 3, 4, and 5, as well as in the newer Phases II and III.

A large mental health facility is also located in the main hospital, supported by several smaller clinics located in Zones 4 and 5. Patients are treated for a variety of mental disorders in these clinics, but the primary complaints tend to be those of depression and post-traumatic stress. One of the Lost Boys by the name of Peter Ajang Awai worked as a mental health counselor at the clinic in Zone 4. Peter, like most of the health-care workers in the camp, is not a qualified doctor or nurse, but rather someone who was selected from among the refugee population and trained in a three-month course. His duties while working at the clinic

91

consisted of writing case reports, disbursing medications such as aspirin, and providing massage therapy, which he used to calm distressed patients.

In addition to the services provided in the clinics, Jesuit Refugee Service (JRS) and Lutheran World Federation (LWF) offer counseling services as well. Daycare centers are also provided where mentally ill patients can be closely monitored between the hours of 7 a.m. to 3 p.m. After that time, the patients are returned to their tukuls and cared for by individuals in the refugee community. Those requiring around-the-clock supervision or more extensive forms of therapy are referred to the mental health facility located in the main hospital. "Doctors are in short supply at the camp," says Peter, who never remembers seeing more than one or two qualified doctors, and only at the main hospital. "Medicines are also in short supply," he says, "or in many cases, nonexistent."

Normal hours of operation for the clinics are from 8 a.m. to 5 p.m. Patients requiring emergency medical treatment after those hours are required to visit the emergency room located in the main hospital in Zone 1. This is no small feat for those living in zones farthest from the hospital, as they have no means of transportation or telephones in which to call for emergency assistance. These patients are required instead to stand by the side of the road until an available IRC vehicle makes its regularly scheduled rounds, occurring approximately every three hours. However, on many occasions the vehicles never come, leaving them stranded by the side of the road or at the mercy of their friends, who must carry them to the hospital if they are unable to walk.

Ever resourceful, the boys accomplish this difficult task by constructing makeshift gurneys in which they tie each corner of a blanket to two long sticks. Depending on the distance they are required to travel, they generally enlist the help of up to ten refugees, enabling each to take a turn in carrying the patient, preventing fatigue or injury to themselves.

Life in general is difficult in Kakuma, where refugees are afforded only the basic essentials necessary for their existence. This extends to their classrooms as well, which were initially held outdoors with minimal shade. Later, under the direction of LWF, mud buildings covered by tin roofs were built, which served as classrooms for both the primary (grades 1-8) and secondary schools (grades 9-12). However, these classrooms remain extremely overcrowded, averaging 100 students per class, and the majority of the teachers are unqualified.

Although the newer classrooms provided moderate shelter from the sun, wind, and rain, they left much to be desired in the way of comfort. Initially, there were no chairs or benches on which the children could sit, so they fashioned their own seats by using mud, shaped into long logs on the floor. In 1993, vocational training schools opened in Kakuma under the direction of Don Bosco, a non-governmental agency, where the boys learned various trades such as tailoring, secretarial skills, plumbing, masonry, and carpentry. Students from the schools eventually used their newly acquired skills to build wooden benches for the secondary school classrooms. Those in the lower grades continue to use the mud logs or benches made from large tree branches that hang from wooden cradles shaped like the letter "Y."

The Christian faith of the boys continues to be a central focus in their lives at Kakuma, as evidenced by their Saturday afternoon gatherings in the empty riverbed that surrounds the camp. Under much-coveted shade from the trees growing along the empty banks, the refugees gather to dance and sing their songs of praise to God. According to aid workers, it's an awesome sight to behold, one that they will most likely never forget. "Even if someone does not believe in our faith," says one Lost Boy, "it will cause them to cry just to witness our love for God." On Sundays, the refugees gather once again for their weekly religious services, normally held in rustic buildings that serve as churches. These buildings are not elaborate places of worship, but rather open-air structures supported by wooden poles and covered with tin roofs. The absence of mud walls allows for occasional breezes to circulate through the crowd of approximately 800 to 1,000 people who gather for such services.

I'm told that the boys built many of the churches, and the fences that surround them, shortly after their arrival at Kakuma. Bishop Nathaniel Garang from the Diocese of Bor in Southern Sudan, who confirmed approximately 10,000 of the Lost Boys following their arrival, chuckles at the memory of the small children carrying large trees on their shoulders to use in building the churches. "They looked like tiny little ants carrying those great big logs," he says. "But they were determined to build their churches." Numerous churches are currently represented in Kakuma, including those from such varied denominations as Catholic, Episcopal, Presbyterian, Pentecostal, and Seventh-Day Adventist. In addition to the numerous Christian churches within the camp, there is a Muslim mosque that is located in the Somali community.

Despite the difficult lifestyle of Kakuma, the years have moved swiftly for the once small boys, who are now teenagers and young men. And as they continue to struggle to make their way in the forsaken place (which they now reluctantly call home), they remain hopeful that they will one day be reunited with their families and friends. In the still night hours, many of the boys feel frightened and alone. Even as young men they continue to yearn for the gentle embrace of their mothers' arms, and their ears are ever on the alert for the sound of their parents' voices calling out their names—calling them home.

The age-old questions never cease: "Why hasn't my family come for me?" "Do they even think of me?" "Are all my loved ones truly dead?" For the majority of the boys, these questions will forever remain unanswered. But they continue to hope, saying they will search for their loved ones until they've taken their very last breath.

For years, the boys shared their stories with foreign journalists and reporters, hoping against all hope that someone would recognize their names and come for them. They've sent desperate pleas around the world for help, praying that someone would rescue them from their despair. But their cries remained unanswered. Many of the boys began to tire of such litanies, saying that it was no use telling their stories because no one in the world was listening.

But then something miraculous happened in 1999 that once again instilled hope in the hearts and minds of the young refugees. News began to travel through the camp that the U.S. government had indeed heard the cry of the Lost Boys and help was on the way.

Working in conjunction with UNHCR and various U.S. resettlement agencies, the U.S. government established a refugee resettlement program, granting approximately 3,800 of the Lost Boys the opportunity of resettling in America. Those selected would be required to complete a mandatory resettlement process, as set forth by the U.S. government and UNHCR, which included medical screening, extensive paperwork, and finally an orientation class to help them better assimilate to their new lives in America.

Mr. Sasha Chanoff, formally of the International Organization of Migration (IOM), arrived in Kakuma in August of 2000 with the assignment of developing the curriculum that was to be used in those orientation classes. In doing so, he grew concerned about the many obstacles the boys might face when arriving to America. He knew that obvious problems would arise due to the cultural differences of the boys, in comparison to those of Americans. But beyond that, he also worried about the reactions of the Lost Boys to Western civilization in general. "How would they differentiate reality from make believe? How would they react to the multitude of mundane daily tasks, such as crossing the street at a traffic light?" Although such tasks were second nature to most Americans, Mr. Chanoff realized that they could, at first, prove overwhelming for the Lost Boys, who had never been exposed to such things.

The boys had only three days in which to unravel the many mysteries that awaited them in America. Three days in which Chanoff must find a way to dispel their preconceived misconceptions, while at the same time address important issues such as employment, money, the roles of resettlement agencies, and the pertinent laws of the US. It was an overwhelming task to say the least, but one which he found to be immensely satisfying.

Due to the large numbers of boys attending the orientation classes, Chanoff says he found it difficult at first to remember their names. However, he quickly remedied the problem, learning to identify them by the shirts that they wore. "It was an easy means of identification," says Chanoff, "because most of them owned only one shirt and they wore it everyday." But their lack of clothing was not the only thing he observed during his stay in Kakuma. Some of the boys were living in such impoverished states that if he had not seen it with his own eyes, it would have been unimaginable. One group of boys, whom he refers to as group #27, lived in such a state of decay that they were forced to seek shelter at their school.

Like Chanoff, the Lost Boys had questions and concerns of their own regarding their new lives in America. For instance, they wanted to know the going rate of a dowry in the U.S. "Will the government give me a loan?" they asked. The boys were also anxious to learn how they should interact with the women in the U.S. But perhaps most heart-rending of all was the question, "How will we live without our people?" they wondered. "We will be very lonely," they concluded.

To help the boys overcome their anticipated loneliness, the elders composed cassette tapes in which they recorded songs in the boys' native tongue. Also included on the tapes were detailed instructions from the elders on how they should conduct themselves while living in the U.S. "Trust in God," their elders instructed, "stay out of trouble, and never forget those you have left behind. Get your education, and then return home quickly so you can help your people."

Having completed the necessary paperwork, medical evaluations, and cultural orientation classes, the boys were left with only one remaining task: saying goodbye to their friends and loved ones. For many, it would prove to be the most difficult task of all.

PETER JAL KOK

NUER REGION

Since fleeing Pugnido in Ethiopia, Peter had been on the run for more than a year. Like much of his life, the journey had been an extremely hard one, filled with danger and loss. But of course, it was not the first time Peter had experienced loss and it would most likely not be the last. Since leaving his Nuer village of Nual, located in the Bentiu region of Southern Sudan (which Peter refers to as the "heart of Southern Sudan"), Peter had lost much. And now, as he prepared to leave his homeland once again and enter the country of Kenya, Peter took count of his blessings. Unlike many others he had known before who had died on their journey to freedom, Peter was about to cross yet another border, as a survivor.

Initially, Peter and the others set up camp in the town of Lokichokio (Loki), where they remained for approximately two months before receiving word that they would soon be transferred to a new location farther south called the Turkana district. "The Kenyan people had a heart for the Lost Boys," says Peter. "They opened a place of refuge for us called the Kakuma Refugee Camp." Upon arrival in Kakuma, the boys were told that they would receive food and shelter, in addition to a safe haven from the GOS. But even more importantly, the Kenyan government promised the boys that they would receive an education.

However, the promises made by the Kenyan government were not well received by many of the boys, who still viewed their new host with great suspicion. Rumors began spreading through the camp like wildfire, reaching mutinous proportions when a large majority of the boys and other refugees refused to board the transport trucks upon their arrival. "People in the camp were saying that the Kenyan government was working with the government of Sudan," says Lost Boy William Kou. "They told us that if we boarded the trucks, we would be taken instead to Khartoum [the capital of Sudan]. We were very afraid by this news, because we knew that it would be bad for us there. Many of our elders were also suspicious and refused to board the trucks." When it seemed that all efforts to persuade the refugees to board the trucks had failed, a top-ranking commander of the SPLA took charge of the situation, demanding that the restless crowd heed his words. "Everything will be alright," he assured them. "Everyone will be safe." And then, as if to reinforce his words, the commander began to load members of his own family onto the trucks. "Do you think I would send my own family first if I did not believe they would be safe? Come and board the trucks for Kakuma." the commander said. "He was a well-respected person in our community," says William, "and when we saw him send his own family ahead of us, we also began to board the trucks."

William and Peter, along with approximately 100 other Lost Boys, were loaded onto the many large, open-roofed trucks sent by the International Committee of the Red Cross. Each truck held the same number of passengers, all of whom were required to stand for the approximately two-hour journey due to a lack of seats. Those standing on the sides of the truck held on to the many harnesses that hung from metal poles along the sides of the roof, while those standing beside and behind them held onto their shoulders. The others soon followed suit. Thankfully (because the trucks had no air conditioning) the open roofs allowed a slight flow of air to circulate above the boys. The metal walls framing the sides of the trucks, however, prevented any hope of a cross breeze or a chance for the boys to view their surroundings as they traveled. But Peter says he didn't need to see the passing scenery, because he had already formed a mental picture of the place he would soon call home. "I thought it would be really nice there," he says. "I pictured very green pastures, with an abundance of good (clean) water to drink. I was really happy to be going to Kakuma." But on reaching his final destination and exiting the secluded truck, Peter's dreams quickly turned to disappointment.

"Kenya is a very beautiful place, with much wildlife," says Peter. "But the place where we were made to stay in Kakuma was a very dry and miserable place with no vegetation. There is nothing pleasing there. The rain comes only two times a year, making the ground to be very dry and dusty. The dust blows every day from 7 a.m. until 4 p.m. Even when we were in school, the dust would blow through the open windows. Sometimes it blew so much that we were forced to hide our faces inside our shirts. Afterwards we had to blow the dust from our papers in order to see them or to write on them. If I were born in that place [Turkana], I would say that God had cursed me." Peter laughs when saying this, but not because he finds his stay there amusing. Rather, he laughs at the cruel joke played on him and others who were made to live in such a desolate and forsaken place. Peter later asked area aid workers (who were primarily Kenyan citizens), "Why did you put us in such a dry and horrible place? Why could we not go where the grass is green and the land is very beautiful?" They answered him by saying, "If we put you in a beautiful place, you would forget your own country. So we put you in this place so that you will never forget your homeland."

Initially, Peter was housed in an open tent with nine other boys. The boys remained in the tent for several months until provided with the necessary supplies to build their own tukuls. Each group of boys was given wood, a piece of plastic sheeting, and palm fronds to be used in constructing their new homes. With the help and guidance of UNHCR aid workers, they built rudimentary huts, which they framed in wood. Having framed their homes, the boys began the process of filling in the walls with mud made from the red Turkana soil and water. They completed the tukuls by wrapping the plastic sheeting on the framed roofs and covering it with palm fronds. The final product was a rather flimsy house, measuring approximately ten to twelve feet on each side, which began to deteriorate and collapse within approximately eight months of being built.

The task of rebuilding new homes was left solely to the young boys, who became extremely inventive and resourceful in their efforts and designs. Using plastic jugs left over from their water rations, along with discarded plastic fuel containers, the boys made waterproof shingles, which they used on the roofs of their tukuls. Cutting and piecing the small pieces of plastic together, like working a jigsaw puzzle, the boys nailed the shingles to the wooden frames of their roofs. The end result was a somewhat durable home, complete with a waterproof ceiling that remained intact for many years to come. But the durability of the homes would not present as big a problem as that of the size of these dwellings. When initially building the tukuls, the boys were still quite young and intent on returning to their villages in Southern Sudan, as they believed that peace would soon be restored in their country. But as each year turned into the next and the small, young boys began to grow into rather tall young men, it became difficult for them to stand fully erect in their tukuls or to walk through the rather low doorways that they had built as children. However, building supplies were almost nonexistent by that time and the boys were forced to make do with what they had.

Peter lived in a group of approximately twenty Lost Boys housed among two tukuls that were built side by side. As the numbers of refugees in Kakuma continued to grow daily, the existing tukuls proved to be insufficient in housing the large influx of people. Therefore, many of the refugees were forced to live outdoors, sleeping on mats made of palm fronds completely exposed to the elements. Some of the refugees preferred the outdoors, as it was much cooler than sleeping inside. Peter, on the other hand, enjoyed the comfort and protection of living indoors and considers himself lucky for being afforded the luxury of doing so.

In order to receive food, each boy was given a ration card similar to that of a social security card, which they had to present each time they received their rations. The cardinal rule in the camp was "no card, no food," and this rule was strictly enforced. If your card was lost or stolen, you were required to report it immediately. In order to receive a new one, you must be able to recite the number, which had been engraved on the lost card. These strict measures were put in place to prevent double rationing, which could easily deplete the sparse and overburdened food supplies. It was also done in an effort to prevent theft of the cards among the refugee boys and the local Turkana people, who were also desperately in need of food. Guards, employed by the Kenyan government, regularly patrolled the food lines to ensure order and compliance with the rules.

To further maintain order among the refugees as they waited in the long and tiresome lines, the women were grouped separately from the men and placed first in line to receive food. This prevented the men from pushing the women out of the way or trying to move ahead of them. As refugees neared the front of the line, they presented their cards to aid workers who in turn marked their names off of the master list. If someone attempted to use their ration card twice or a card belonging to someone else, guards were quickly alerted and typically responded by throwing the offenders to the ground, while kicking and stomping on them. The perpetrators were then transported by truck to an outside holding area enclosed by a wire fence where they remained for at least four hours in the hot Kenyan sun. Most of the refugees did their best to avoid such punishment, choosing instead to comply with the rules.

Initially each refugee received two cups of lentils, approximately five pounds each of corn and wheat flour, one cup of salt, and one cup of oil. This amount of food would have been more than adequate to sustain a person for a day. But the rations were supposed to last for sometimes 15 to 30 days, depending on the available amounts of food. Typically the food ran out before the next rations came, leaving the boys hungry and empty-handed once again. In addition to their food supplies, the boys received one gallon of water, which they used for cooking, drinking, and bathing. Unlike their food rations, water was generally given daily, but on many occasions it was unavailable and the boys were forced to wait up to 24 hours or longer before receiving water. During these times, the boys kept an open ear while sleeping, listening in earnest for the sounds of the water pumps that signaled that water was once again available. The time of night made little difference to the thirsty boys, who at the sound of the pumps quickly formed lines to receive their water rations. Of course, the water was not purified and required boiling before drinking, but this did not deter the boys. Following the necessary steps of purification, they quickly gulped the soothing liquid, bringing temporary relief to their parched throats and dehydrated bodies.

The boys quickly learned to conserve their food supplies by pooling their rations together and eating only once a day. They selected one boy from each group and assigned him the task of "cooking detail." This assignment was rotated daily and was not a chore to be taken lightly. "If it was your day to do the cooking, you must take your job seriously or the others would be very angry with you," says Peter. "Even if you were playing soccer or studying your assignments for school, you must stop what you were doing and begin the necessary preparations for the evening meal."

Those preparations included gathering (or purchasing when necessary) the needed firewood to be used in cooking the meal. The boys typically made soups or porridge from water and any other ingredients that were available at the time. On rare occasions those ingredients included fresh meat, but meat was available only to a select few within the camp—mainly those refugees working for the various relief agencies or those extremely motivated and inventive in their efforts to earn money. Peter and his roommates fell into the latter category with several of them earning incomes on a regular basis. Although they were unable to obtain jobs with the various non-governmental organizations, they were not deterred and became extremely entrepreneurial in their own efforts to create a source of income. The work was hard and the rewards were generally small, but the boys had one thing on their side—time—and they had plenty of it.

Peter worked only when needing to buy something of importance, such as clothing, food, or extra pens and pencils for school. Although the boys were given pencils and pens at the onset of the school year by the country of Japan, if they were lost, stolen, or broken, it was the responsibility of the boys to obtain new ones. In order to do so, the boys either had to barter something of value for the needed items or purchase them from one of the local markets. Like Japan, other countries also donated supplies and food to the refugees with each of the items bearing the name of the country that had donated it. This made for easy identification of the various countries around the world that had helped to assist the Lost Boys in their time of need. And later, when food supplies began dwindling within the camp, it was easy to identify these items when they began to show up in the local Kenyan markets. Dishonest government officials or bandits patrolling the roadsides often confiscated the donated food while it was en route to the camp and sold it for a profit. Many times, the boys saw flour and corn for sale in the market stalls with the words "Donated by USA" clearly printed on the bags.

Without any means of recourse, Peter and his roommates devised their own plan for supplementing their minimal rations, which eventually enabled them to purchase other needed items as well. "If I needed something like school supplies or extra clothing," says Peter, "I would first meet with my housemates and ask for their permission to use some of our rations to obtain the items. If they agreed, I was granted their permission." Peter did not require much, however, as he had a gift for turning the smallest of loan into a considerably large return on his investment. Although still a young boy, Peter was incredibly inventive in devising such plans. "We saved a portion of our oil until the end of the month when rations in the camp began to disappear," he explained. "At that time, after finishing my schooling for the day, I went to make business. I took one cup of oil to the most expensive market in Kakuma or the surrounding area and I sold it for a very good price. I then traveled by foot to another market in the camp where the price of oil was much less. Kakuma is a very big place; it could take thirty minutes to three hours to reach such a market by foot. I then purchased two cups of oil at the cheaper market for the same price that I had sold the first. Afterward, I traveled back to the first market, or one that was closer, which also paid high prices for the oil, and I sold those two cups of oil for a very good price." Peter continued the same process until raising the amount of money that he needed.

As an additional source of income, Peter also established a part-time "bicycle taxi service." "Sometimes people needed to reach an area of the camp that was very far away or they wished to take a bus someplace and needed transportation to reach the bus station. I rented a bicycle from one of my friends for sixty cents a day and then used the bicycle to transport those people to their destinations." Peter charged his clients approximately twenty to thirty cents per fifteen minutes of travel and increased his earnings by taking multiple people at one time. The bicycle had a large seat (similar to what Americans once called banana seats) that would accommodate two people, Peter and another. There was room for an additional person on the handlebars and yet another (or a piece of luggage) on the cross bar that extended from the handlebars to the seat. The bicycle taxi service was a strenuous job, requiring considerable talent in order to maneuver the bike over rough terrain. Although Peter felt fortunate to make the approximate two dollars and forty cents he cleared each day after paying his rental fee, he did this job only until earning the exact amount of money that he needed. "I was still very young and did not have the strength to work for long periods of time in those conditions. It was very hot and dusty and I sometimes worked so hard that I became weak and started urinating blood. It was really, really bad," Peter remembers, bowing his head to hide his face.

Others, like Peter's housemate B'bol (pronounced Bee-bull), did not have the option of choosing whether or not to work. Not only had B'bol become separated from his parents due to the war in Sudan, but he had also inherited the responsibility of raising his younger brother James (typically pronounced Jame-is by the Lost Boys). In addition to providing his younger brother with food and shelter, B'bol felt the responsibility to provide him with a proper education as well. And although there were schools in Kakuma, the teachers often lacked professional training. The nearby Kenyan schools, located outside the camp, were far superior, but they also came with a substantial price tag. Again, only a select few of the refugees were able to afford such schools, and B'bol was determined to be one of them. In order to achieve that goal, he remembers selling his only pair of shoes to buy an extra bag of flour at the market. However, the flour would not be consumed by B'bol, nor his brother or house-mates. It was used instead for the initial start-up capital for a new business venture that he had in mind.

B'bol used the flour to make a round, flat bread (also called paper food) with the intention of selling it to the local people surrounding the camp, aid workers, and those few refugees who were able to afford it. He in turn used the profits that he made from selling the bread to purchase additional flour. Soon his reputation for making the tasty bread grew, as did his profits, enabling B'bol to raise the needed money to build a small hut, which served as a restaurant. New items were soon added to the menu, including soups and tea. In no time at all, his eating establishment became a favorite among locals, and the number of clientele surpassed that of other restaurants in the camp. But his good fortune came with great sacrifice, as his daily preparations began at 4 a.m. and continued until closing the restaurant at 11 p.m. On a good day he cleared around $100 US dollars, but on average his return was only $50 US dollars or less. Not bad for a young businessman who was only 15 or 16 years old at the time! The typical menu at B'bol's restaurant was:

Bean soup – Ten cents US
Vegetable soup – Ten cents US
Meat soup – Twenty-five cents US
A cup of tea – Five cents US
Paper food (bread) – Thirteen cents per piece (measuring approximately 12-24 inches round)

Against all odds, Peter and his roommates were earning a living in the worst economy imaginable, knowing that their future depended upon their success—a future that was coming much too quickly for young boys who were resigned to the fact that they would most likely remain in Kakuma for the rest of their lives, or until they were forced to return to the horrors of their homeland. "There was no happiness in our lives," says Peter. "When we were living in Kakuma, we were confined to a place with no movement. There was no freedom to move outside the confines of the camp unless you obtained the necessary documentation from the UN, but even then, sometimes we were refused. We were then forced to go to the local Kenyan police station and bribe someone. Everything is about bribery in Kenya. After leaving the first police station, we were sent to the next one on our route where we were once again forced to bribe someone. We traveled from one police station to the next along our journey, bribing someone at each stop, until reaching our final destination. When it was time to return to Kakuma, we were forced to repeat the process all over again."

Although Peter could not begin to understand the reasons why he had been placed in such conditions, or why his path was so different from others around the world, he gradually began to accept his life as his predetermined fate. He trusted God to provide for him in all ways, and even in the worst of circumstances, his faith in God remained unwavering. But unbeknownst to Peter, he was about to reach a fork in the middle of the road on which he had long traveled. When doing so, he was faced with the choice of a different path that would lead him to a future beyond that which he could have ever imagined. Peter explains it like this: "God prepared a different way for me." And indeed, He did.

In August of 1999, unannounced and without warning, UN officials came for Peter with some very shocking news. "It was a miracle, truly," says Peter. Peter was among the first group of boys to arrive in Kakuma back in 1992, and therefore his name had been selected for a new refugee resettlement program. This program, he was told, would take place in a country located far away from his homeland, but to his relief, walking would not be the method of transportation. In fact, this country was so far away that it was not reachable even by truck. If selected, Peter would be living on another continent, in a country called the "United States of America."

Peter had studied about the U.S. in school and had seen its name stamped upon many of the donated items in the camp. He was excited at the prospect of going there, but that excitement was soon squelched by others in the camp, such as the Kenyans and Turkanas, who were resentful of the boys. They began to fill his ears with stories of woe in an effort to dissuade him from leaving the camp if his name was selected. "If you marry a girl in the U.S.," they told him, "she will have many boyfriends. If she tells you that one of her boyfriends is coming to visit her, you will have to leave your own home until he is gone." They had the most impact, however, when telling Peter that the Sudanese government had actually sold him illegally to the U.S. They told him that if he went to America he would become a slave and he would be forced to clean the teeth of donkeys. Peter had heard many stories about people who had been captured in the south of Sudan and sold into slavery. He became frightened by the possibility that this could happen to him as well. In fact, he became so frightened that he contemplated remaining in Kakuma and refusing to go to America if his name was selected.

But shortly thereafter, a Lost Boy who had resettled in the U.S. through different channels contacted Peter. The boy was a trusted friend of Peter and he listened to him as he told a different version of America than that of the Kenyans and Turkanas. "Don't be discouraged," he told Peter. "America is beautiful and the people are very friendly. It is a wonderful place to live." By the end of their conversation, Peter's mind was finally made up and his decision was final: If given the chance to live in America, his answer would be "yes." In fact, Peter was so hopeful at the prospect of going to the U.S. that he began praying to God, asking Him to make a way for him to do so as soon as possible.

But in the meantime, there was much to be done. Certain obligations had to be fulfilled before his allotted time of departure, such as U.S. Immigration and Naturalization Service interviews and the completion of endless amounts of paperwork. New photos were required since the previous ones were almost two years old and no longer considered valid. Medical examinations must also be performed to ensure that the boys were healthy and able to travel, confirming also that they were free from HIV or other infectious diseases.

With all his obligations finally fulfilled, the only thing left for Peter to do was wait...

Communication was difficult in the camp, as there were no phones except pay phones located in the main area of the camp. The only means of announcing the names that had been selected for resettlement was by posting them on a white wooden signboard located near the main entrance of the camp. The boys simply referred to it as "the board." Peter was fortunate in that the board was only a two-minute journey from his tukul, while others in the camp were required to travel great distances in order to search for their names. Visiting the board became a regular stop in Peter's daily routine, where he searched diligently for his name. But each day Peter was met with disappointment when his name did not appear on the list of those selected. He was determined to remain hopeful, however, even as the passing days since first learning of his chance for resettlement had turned into months and eventually years.

And then one day in August of 2001, almost two years later, Peter was greeted by his housemate Stephen Wan as he walked home from school. Stephen was very excited, telling Peter that he had seen his name listed on the board. Peter could hardly believe his ears and quickly ran to see for himself. Sure enough, there it was in black and white: Peter Jal Kok. Also listed were the state and city in which Peter would be living. He took note that he would be living in a place called "Jacksonville, Florida." Added to his excitement was another familiar name on the list, that of his good friend and housemate Stephen Deng, who would also be residing in Jacksonville. This was cause for celebration indeed!

Although the names of everyone living in Peter's group had initially been submitted for consideration, Peter and Stephen were the only two who had been selected from their group. They had all arrived in Kakuma at the same time, but their names were selected randomly and everyone was subject to the luck of the

104

draw. On that particular day, some would say that Lady Luck had smiled on Peter and Stephen, granting them their good fortune. To Peter, it was only God who had miraculously answered his prayers.

Peter and Stephen's housemates joined in their excitement and began collecting monetary contributions toward a special meal in their honor. Each boy donated approximately fifty cents of his hard-earned money to be used toward the purchase of meat and other delicacies to be served in the celebration feast. The women living in close proximity to their tukuls were also invited. "Someone had to cook the special foods. Our cooking was not so good!" smiles Peter. "So we invited the women to do all of the cooking for us!"

Each boy was required to attend a three-day orientation class in an effort to prepare him for his final journey from the Stone Age of Africa to the 21st century of America. However, nothing could truly prepare these boys for the new sights and wonders they were about to see and experience. On August 5, 2001, the plane that was to transport them on the first part of their journey to America landed in the Kakuma Refugee Camp. As Peter walked up the narrow ramp leading into the plane, he felt excited and happy to be leaving Kakuma. "I knew that I would never miss that place," he says. But as he turned, looking back down the ramp, he caught one last glimpse of the young men with whom he had shared so much. Those he had walked beside through the wilds of Africa, those he had run beside while being chased by enemy soldiers, those with whom he had almost starved and endured more hardships than anyone could ever imagine. And as he looked into their faces, the faces of his brothers with whom he had survived against all odds, his heart was heavy and his eyes filled with tears. Yes, he was leaving Africa, but he knew that his heart would always remain there, with the people that he knew and loved.

With the exception of B'bol's younger brother James, all of the boys featured in this book were eventually selected as well. Many others, however, were left behind and given no promises regarding their own fate. But they were encouraged by the fact that so many of their friends had been selected, and for the first time in many years a new spark of hope was kindled within them—hope that one day their own names would also appear on the board and they would join their friends and relatives in America.

Riding on the plane was a new and strange adventure for the boys. "When the plane took off, I felt as if my heart had fallen back to the ground," says Peter. "It was really incredible!" The boys experienced many new things on their journey to America, the first of which was airline food. "I did not know how to eat this food because everything was wrapped up separately. I did not know where to begin," he laughs. "There were journalists aboard the plane who were filming us and I didn't want to look stupid, like I didn't know anything. So I watched the man sitting next to me. I think he was European or something. I glanced over at him when no one was looking to see what he was doing with his food. And whatever I saw him doing, I did it also. And that is how I learned to eat food on an airplane."

News also began to travel throughout the airplane regarding an exciting discovery in the rear of the plane. There was a real flushing toilet in the bathroom! Peter had heard about such things in his orientation class, and he decided to put some of his newly acquired knowledge to work. He boldly walked to the rear of the plane ready to experience the flushing toilet for the first time. When doing so he was quite surprised. "I didn't realize it would be so loud!" he exclaims. "It made a very terrible noise and frightened me." But Peter adds that the flushing toilet fascinated him nonetheless.

The plane stopped for a short time in Brussels, Belgium, before landing in the U.S., and the boys suddenly found themselves surrounded by more white people than they had ever seen. To the boys it seemed that there were no black people in Belgium, only the people with white skin. "Who are you boys? Where do you come from?" they wanted to know. "Are you on a team? What team do you play on?" The Lost Boys had no idea what they were talking about.

After a brief layover in Belgium, the boys boarded yet another plane before continuing on their journey to the U.S. "This was the scariest part of the trip," remembers Peter, "because when the plane flew over the Atlantic Ocean it began to go up and then come down again. It kept doing this over and over again, up and down, up and down. Some of the boys became very sick with the vomiting and we were all really scared. It was at this time that we pulled our covers over our heads and refused to look around us."

Shortly thereafter, the captain's voice sounded over the plane's intercom, signaling the end of their long journey and the final descent into New York City's JFK airport. As the wheels of the plane touched down on the runway, the passengers responded with the sound of thunderous applause in tribute to their captain for a job well done. The captain responded in kind, his long-awaited words resonating through the cabin: "Welcome to America!"

Lost Boys reading at Kakuma

Lost Boys make toys from soda cans to imitate U.N. trucks and planes

107

Lost Boys playing a form of Sudanese soccer

Lost Boys arrive to Kakuma in 1992

Lost Boys construct tukuls after arriving in Kakuma to 1992

UNHCR/J. Ghedini/2004

Kakuma

Melanie & Roy Sasscer

Church at Alpha Kakuma with mud seats

Sign at Kakuma

The Cost of Liberty
by Awer G. Bul

111

"Give me your tired, your poor,

Your huddled masses

Yearning to breathe free."

Emma Lazarus

WELCOME
TO
AMERICA!

The flight to freedom was a similar one for most of the Lost Boys, all of whom were equally fascinated by the strange foods and the roaring toilets filled with mysterious blue waters that, with a touch of a handle, suddenly vanished into a dark hole appearing from nowhere. Added to the many wonders was the frightening force of the turbulent winds that tossed their planes up and down, creating panic in some who feared they might fall into the ocean or be smashed against the mighty mountains looming just outside their cabin windows. Little did they know that this incredible adventure would be only one of many that awaited them once they arrived in the U.S.

Upon departing the plane and entering JFK airport in New York City, the Lost Boys found themselves surrounded by a multitude of new sights, sounds, and smells. Many of the things that we as Americans take for granted both frightened and fascinated them—especially the moving stairs that seemed to magically transport them from up to down and down to up, making it appear as if they were floating through the air. Peter had a near-death experience on such stairs, saying that when he stepped onto them the ground beneath him suddenly disappeared. Thrown off balance, he screamed in fright as he began to fall forward. "Had the man behind me not grabbed my shirt and pulled me back to safety," declares Peter, "I would have truly died on that day from the big fall."

After clearing immigration and customs, the boys continued on their journeys and arrived at their predetermined destinations, which they now called "home." Funding provided in part by the U.S. government, and by agencies such as Lutheran Social Services, Catholic Charities, and World Relief, assisted them during their resettlement process. Private citizens also rallied around the boys becoming not only their mentors, but also their surrogate mothers and fathers. These volunteers came from all walks of life, bringing with them a vast array of unique talents and gifts.

The first groups of boys to arrive in Jacksonville were sponsored primarily by Lutheran Social Services (LSS). In an effort to make their transition a smooth one, LSS provided them with two caseworkers, George Aweet and Rachel Obal, both of whom were also from Sudan and able to communicate with the boys in Arabic and Dinka. Initially, Rachel held daily orientation classes which were mandatory for the boys to attend. Various speakers were invited to these classes, such as college professors, law enforcement officials, and bankers, in an attempt to better educate the boys on the laws and customs in America. Field trips were also included, allowing the boys the opportunity to familiarize themselves with the numerous sites and layout of the large city. The beach quickly became a favorite spot. On their first trip there, they simply shed their clothes as they had done when swimming in the rivers and streams of Africa and jumped naked into the water.

At first, the boys were placed in one- and two-bedroom apartments in groups of two to six boys per apartment. (Most prefer to remain in these large group settings even today.) Living conditions were cramped to say the least and the apartments were minimally furnished. But to these young men who had spent so many years roaming the wilds of Africa or living in refugee camps, they were "Paradise." Their first month's rent was paid by LSS with the second month's rent typically provided by the individual apartment complexes. At the end of those two months, however, the boys were responsible for paying their own rent and utilities.

Their personal belongings were meager, generally consisting of one pair of shorts or pants, a t-shirt, and a worn-out pair of flip-flops. But no matter how few their possessions, they were always willing to share them if asked. I remember taking pictures of a group of boys one day (they love to have their pictures taken) to send back to their friends and family in Africa. Only one of the boys owned a pair of closed-toe shoes and although they were obviously second-hand, he proudly shared them with the others. As each boy was photographed, he donned the prized shoes, caring little if they were too small or too large, passing them on to the next person in line when finished. I was so touched by the pride they exuded in wearing the worn-out shoes that I immediately felt guilty for the many things I had long taken for granted in my own life. I walked away that day feeling thankful for my many blessings. I think most people who meet the Lost Boys walk away with that same sense of appreciation.

In addition to clothing, they needed various household items such as cooking utensils and furniture. Because of limited space, many of them shared their beds with others; but in light of the fact that these were the first real beds (with mattresses) that most of them had ever slept on, they didn't seem to mind. I remember the first time I showed some of them how to sleep under a soft blanket. For many, their previous beds had been straw mats that lay on the hard dusty ground or worn-out cots. As each boy took his turn lying under the blanket, he and the others began to chatter excitedly in their native tongue. And then in a grand finale, they began to cluck like chickens. It's actually a clicking sound that some of them make with their tongues when they become excited or awed by something. It sounds similar to the noise one makes when calling a horse, but in their native country it is the equivalent of saying "Wow!" or "Awesome!" Imagine their response when laying their heads on a soft down pillow for the very first time—yep, there was a lot of clucking going on that day!

Eventually the boys were provided with all the essential items they needed and in most cases much more. Of course, then began the arduous task of teaching them how to use the various items. Initially, they required instruction in the simplest of tasks—how to use a can opener, eat with utensils, vacuum the floor, wash dishes (with soap), and even how to hang their clothes on little wire things that we know as "coat hangers." The need for them to learn such things, at their ages, is perhaps what so endeared them to us as volunteers. But they were fast learners, eagerly soaking up all information given them like a dry sponge. In no time at all, they were adapting to Western civilization, and some became extremely "Americanized" in the process. The desire to succeed at all cost became overpowering for many of them, who initially spent their Saturday and Sunday afternoons on the soccer field or in church, but eventually devoted their entire weekends and all free time to school and work. And while it has been truly inspiring to witness the incredible speed in which they have adjusted to their new lives here in America, my pride and appreciation for their accomplishments are often laced with sadness at the disappearance of their childlike innocence. I can't help but wonder what such changes might cost them in the long run.

I remember watching a Lost Boy one day as he danced beside his car to the beat of an American song blaring from his car stereo. His moves were strictly American in origin, most likely copied from MTV or BET, both popular channels among the boys. As I continued to watch him, an unexpected sadness swept over me at the realization that he had indeed become "Americanized." And although I had often encouraged him and others to adapt to our customs in hopes that it would help them to better succeed in our society, at that particular moment, I paused to consider what impact such changes may have on their future generations. *Will they eventually abandon the ways of their ancestors and choose to raise their children instead in accordance with American values and traditions?* I wondered.

But then, as if reading my thoughts, the Lost Boy suddenly switched gears, moving instead to the rhythm of his native dance, jumping through the air in spectacular movements mastered only by his people. And then, just in case there were any lingering doubts left in my mind, he began to trill his voice in the triumphant yell of his ancestors, signaling to me, as well as the rest of the world, that his tribal roots remained firmly in place.

For the first eight months following their arrival, or until gainfully employed, each of the boys was to receive $120 US dollars in food stamps along with an additional $180 US dollars in public assistance. Medicaid benefits were also provided during this time in addition to transportation to and from their medical appointments. And although they were extremely grateful for the generosity extended to them by our government, the majority of the boys took little satisfaction in receiving the assistance, saying that they preferred to earn their money instead. Some were able to secure jobs rather quickly, but they were typically temporary positions, ending almost as soon as they began and resulting in the loss of their government assistance. The process for reinstating their assistance was often a long one that in many cases took months, leaving the boys without sufficient means of support except for the assistance they received from LSS, fellow Lost Boys, and generous volunteers.

Typically, LSS moved quickly to find employment for new refugees, but due to the circumstances surrounding these young men, special considerations had to be made. Without prior job experience, the majority of them lacked the skills needed to function in the American workforce. Most had not yet completed high school and were under the false assumption that upon arriving in America, the only task required of them would be their daily attendance in school. And while that assumption may have been a valid one for those living in other states who had been deemed "unaccompanied minors," it was not the case for those living in Jacksonville who were 21 or older. The young men living in our city were considered adults and therefore were expected to live independently in a very short period of time. But after working with them through the years, I have often questioned the ages given them, believing some of them to be much younger. However, volunteers generally do not challenge this issue for fear that the boys will be accused of entering our country fraudulently and consequently be deported.

Before long, other problems began to surface, such as the boys' apparent difficulty with managing their time. Not only were the majority of them late for pre-scheduled appointments and meetings, but also in many cases they failed to show up at all. With much of their lives having been spent in upheaval, never knowing from one day until the next where they might be at any given time, they adopted a very noncommittal, laid-back way of living: "Maybe I will be there, maybe I will not." This is also because the majority of them never owned watches or clocks before coming to the U.S., nor had they ever held jobs requiring them to be in a specific place at a specific time. As a result, punctuality has

116

never been one of their strong points.

And although this part of their otherwise wonderful personalities has proved very frustrating for volunteers, the Lost Boys were shocked to learn that such behavior was considered rude or inconsiderate by Americans. To them, it was simply their way of life, an accepted part of their culture. And while many of them have abandoned this lifestyle, realizing that it may result in the loss of employment or the assistance of volunteers, for many it remains a problem, as old habits are hard to break.

Equally difficult is their weakness in communication skills, not only with volunteers, but also among themselves. In all fairness, this is probably due to barriers of their language to some degree, but even more so to their culture. As a result, it is not unusual for one of them to move to another state without saying goodbye to their "brothers" or to their volunteers, as a transient lifestyle is commonly accepted and practiced among them.

Because of these issues, I and others learned early on that it served little purpose to leave a message for one of them with their housemates or friends, because the message would most likely never be delivered. In fact, at times it seems that these young men never tell each other anything.

As an example, some of the volunteers, including myself, planned a birthday party for a group of them at one of their apartments to celebrate their first birthdays in the U.S. We had planned this party for weeks, coordinating our efforts with a Lost Boy named Peter who lived in the apartment where the party was to be held. Peter was generally home during the day and easily reached, so he seemed the perfect person with whom to coordinate our efforts and relay the party information to the others. We were expecting approximately 50 young men to attend this party, so as a precaution I called their apartment several hours beforehand to ensure that we had enough chairs for everyone.

"Hello," a voice answered. "Hi, Richard! It's Mama Joan. I just want to make sure that we have enough chairs for the big party tonight." "What party is that?" he asked. "You know, the party we're having at your house in a couple of hours." "We're having a party here?" "Yes, didn't Peter tell you?" "No, he did not tell me about a party." "Well, we're having one and it's at your apartment. We're expecting about 50 guys." There was a brief pause, followed by a loud discussion in Dinka in the background. Finally, Richard returned to inform me that no one in his apartment knew anything about a party. "You mean 50 guys are coming to your apartment in two hours and you don't even know about it?! Where is Peter?" I asked. "He is out." "Where did he go?" "He did not say." "Is he coming back soon?" "I don't know this." *Of course not,* I thought, *because that would require the two of you to actually communicate with one another!*

Eventually I became so frustrated that I finally asked them, "How is it that every time I see you guys you're talking a hundred miles a minute in your native language, yet you never seem to tell each other anything? What in the world are you talking about all the time?!" Of course my question went unanswered, save their unanimous laughter, as no one seemed able to talk about it! I'd like to say that they have since cleared this hurdle, but it seems as though they are only halfway around the track. The good news, however, is that they are finally running in the right direction, and with each passing day they continue to gain speed. I hope that in mentioning this small part of their personality that I have not belittled them in any way. I respect them far too much for that. It is simply a part of who they are and how they live.

Some people may be fooled by the fact that the Lost Boys are from rural Africa and have received only minimal education, thinking that they are of lower intelligence. But this would be a gross error in judgment, as the majority of them have proven to be extremely intelligent, averaging straight A's in school or the 4.0 GPA equivalent. The Lost Boys, who once claimed that "an education was their only mother and father," are extremely dedicated not only to receiving an education, but also to performing at the highest academic level possible. Following an exam his first semester in college, Abraham Chol was asked by a mentor how he had done. "Horrible!" he exclaimed. "I almost flunked it." "Oh my," said the mentor, "what on earth did you make?" "I made a B!" "Well, a B is a good grade," she told him. "No," said Abraham, "I must make the A's."

Some of the boys passed their General Education Development (GED) test within the first year of their arrival, earning a diploma equivalent to that received when graduating from high school. Some of these remarkable young men, who speak as many as five languages, are currently studying to become doctors, surgeons, accountants, and lawyers among other professional careers, with several having earned places on the dean's list and president's clubs at their colleges.

However, those fortunate enough to attend college often do so at extreme sacrifice, sleeping as little as two hours a night due to class assignments and work schedules. They are driven not only by their own desires to succeed, but also by the knowledge that the survival of so many is dependent upon their success. In addition to the inherited financial obligations for their birth siblings, many are equally responsible for the welfare of their stepsiblings, produced by their father's additional wives. Also factored into the burdensome equation are surviving parents, cousins, aunts, uncles, and close friends, none of whom are afraid to ask for money.

In fact, the Lost Boys receive endless phone calls at all hours of the night, filled with urgent requests from their friends and family in Africa. Some of them have become extremely troubled by these calls, feeling an overwhelming sense of guilt at their inability to meet the needs of so many. One of the boys told me that several of his brothers owed dowries totaling $50,000 US dollars, and should he fail to send the money, his brothers faced the possible confiscation of their children by their wives' families.

One can only imagine the pressure that such demands place on these young men, who are still desperately struggling to make their way in a strange and foreign country. Some, in an effort to meet the overwhelming obligations expected of them, have been forced to hold an additional full- or part-time job, thereby eliminating all hope of an education. Others, in an effort to escape the constant pleas for money, have installed caller IDs on their phones or have changed their numbers to unpublished listings. In taking such measures, they have not in any way relinquished their responsibilities, but have instead given themselves the liberty of contributing only if and when they are able to. Needless to say, this has been a huge change of plans for some Lost Boys, who originally came to our country for the sole purpose of gaining an education.

For many of the Lost Boys, America has not been the "Promised Land" that they were expecting. Much to their disappointment, there are no streets paved with gold, no big houses with their names written on them, and no trees with an abundance of money growing on them. Although initially supported by our government and various resettlement agencies, the Lost Boys no longer receive funding from those agencies. The generous contributions and moral support of volunteers and mentors have also dwindled, as many of them have resumed caring for their own families and financial obligations. For the first time in most of their lives, the Lost Boys, long dependent on the gifts of others, are now faced with the overwhelming task of making it on their own in this strange country.

Yes, life is turning out to be pretty tough in the land of opportunity, but one thing is certain: They have been through much worse and survived. There is little doubt that these remarkable young men—who in their short lifetimes have survived starvation, disease, separation from their parents, lions, and war—will survive in America as well.

There are many stories to tell about their struggles in America, many of which I've included in the final portion of this chapter in the form of vignettes. Some are touching, while others are quite humorous. In sharing these stories with you, it is not at all my intention to disrespect these incredible young men whom I love so much. But rather to give you, the reader, a better insight into the daily struggles of refugees entering our country. I hope you enjoy reading them as much as I've enjoyed experiencing them.

"THIS IS THE SUDANESE NASCAR TEAM."

As I mentioned earlier, the Lost Boys faced numerous obstacles when seeking employment, but the issue of transportation was probably the most significant. Because they had never driven cars before coming to the U.S., they had no experience or knowledge of how to do so. As a result, they were able to accept only those jobs reachable by bicycle, on foot, or through the use of public transportation. (I have often wondered why our government does not include driver education courses as a part of its resettlement program, as many refugees from third-world countries have never driven cars before coming to America. Most new arrivals cannot afford the expensive fees for these courses, but quickly learn that they will be unable to obtain jobs without means of transportation. And thus a continuous cycle of unemployment follows.)

Most of the boys preferred to walk or ride their bikes to work rather than using the public bus service, for fear that they would become lost en route. In many cases, they relied instead on volunteers to take them to and from their places of employment. Needless to say, purchasing cars of their own became a top priority among the boys. But before doing so, they had to learn how to drive, and that was no easy task for them or the volunteers who were brave enough to teach them. I knew early on that it was not my gift, but I feel compelled to give the following suggestions to anyone who feels it may be his or hers:

1. Pray.
2. Increase the liability, personal injury, and collision coverage on your insurance policy.
3. Pray.
4. Fasten your seatbelts securely.
5. Pray.
6. Install air bags throughout the inside perimeter of your car.
7. And last but not least, pray, giving thanks for having survived the ordeal.

We've received numerous phone calls regarding Lost Boys behind the wheels of cars, ultimately earning them the reputation of "demolition derby wannabes." The manager of one apartment complex where I frequently volunteered called me on a regular basis to report accidents involving the Sudanese NASCAR team. Typically her calls went something like this: "Joan, I just want to let you know that one of the Lost Boys drove into his apartment building today while trying to learn how to drive. I don't think any serious damage was done, but could you please ask him to practice somewhere else?" Or "Hi Joan, I just thought I should let you know that one of the Lost Boys ran into a traffic light today and knocked it over. No charges were pressed against him, but he did get a little banged up and one of the other boys took him to the emergency room."

On one occasion she even called to report an accident involving her own vehicle. "Where did it happen?" I asked. "Oh, it happened in the complex parking lot." "Did he hit you when you were pulling out of your parking place or something?" "Oh, no, nothing like that." "Well, did he hit you as he was driving around the corner? Maybe he didn't see you—where were you?" "Well, I was sitting at my desk inside my office and my car was parked out front in plain sight. He just smashed right into it." "Oh," I said. And then not really knowing what else to say, I offered a simple, "Oops!"

But I think my all-time favorite Lost Boy driving story is that of John Dau, who after receiving his much-coveted driver's license promptly purchased his first new car. Well, it wasn't actually new, it was used, but it was bright red and it glimmered in the afternoon sun like polished diamonds. John loved that car with all his heart, which perhaps explains his distress over wrecking it only one hour after having bought it. Seeing the badly damaged car, volunteer Ray Storms (whom the boys call Papa Ray) asked John what had happened. "Did you forget which pedal was the brake and which was the gas?" he asked. "Well, Papa Ray," John explained, "you know how the Lost Boys like to hear the car engines go 'vroom, vroom'? I tried to do this, but I pressed on the gas pedal thinking that the car was in park and actually it was in drive." This error in John's judgment resulted in a face-to-face encounter between his beloved car and a large concrete block wall—which, by the way, was the only thing separating his car from the living room of his apartment. His roommates later teased him, saying that it was his intention to create a drive-in living room.

John, on the other hand, was devastated after damaging his beloved car and implored Papa Ray to fix it. "Jack-of-All-Trades" Papa Ray promised to do his best and promptly headed to the auto salvage yard with Lost Boy Abraham Chol in tow to assist in the search for needed parts. Upon arriving at the salvage yard, Abraham was in awe at the many cars piled one on top of the other and he asked Papa Ray, "Where did all of these cars come from?" With tongue in cheek and a coy smile on his face, Papa Ray replied, "Oh, they came from Lost Boys learning how to drive."

I'm happy to report that everyone in Jacksonville has survived the Lost Boys' road show to date, and that for the most part, the boys have since become safe and conscientious drivers. However, I can't say the same about their cars, or those of their instructors, many of which also now lie in piles at the auto salvage yard.

"WE DON'T HAVE THESE."

In addition to the issue of transportation was that of their health and overall stamina. Initially, a local division of a national delivery service employed a group of the boys, graciously taking them under their wings. Some of the employees even collected money to purchase the required work boots for the boys. At first it seemed as if they had found the perfect job, but shortly thereafter, the boys began quitting for no apparent reason.

Both the volunteers and management were perplexed by their actions and perhaps somewhat perturbed, as no explanation was given. I finally confronted one of them one day and asked him why he and the others had quit such a wonderful job. With shoulders dropped and eyes cast down, he tried to explain. "Mama Joan," he said, "we quit this job because we lack something essential to our success." And then holding his stick thin left arm in front of him, he wrapped the fingers of his right hand around his left bicep saying, "You must have muscles to do this job. And we don't have these." I felt horrible for not realizing sooner the real reason why they had quit their jobs. It wasn't because they were lazy or unappreciative, but rather because after a lifetime of suffering and starvation, the work required of them was more than their frail bodies could withstand.

Added to their physical limitations was their apparent anxiety when meeting new people or visiting strange places. There was also a tendency among them to take everything they heard or saw at face value, which combined to create considerable confusion and misunderstanding.

When I heard that another group of boys had also quit their jobs, I asked them why. In loud and excited tones, they told me that their employers were trying to kill them. "What makes you think that?" I asked. "They force us to work with poisonous chemicals!" "What kind of chemicals?" "Chemicals that can result in our death!" they exclaimed. "Who told you that?" "We know this to be true, because we read it on the labels." I was somewhat alarmed by what I was hearing, but somewhat leery as well, knowing that they tended to overreact or misinterpret things. "What are the names of these chemicals?" I asked. "Blitch," they spat out. *Blitch?* I thought. *What in the world is that?* Suddenly it dawned me, and I asked if they meant to say "bleach." "Yes," they said, happy to know that I was finally on the same page as they were. And then, in an attempt to further impress me with their newfound knowledge they asked, "Mama Joan, did you know that blitch can even cause blindness?"

Of course, when learning of their employer's sinister plot to kill them, they did what was only natural when threatened with their lives—they walked... right out the door, never looking back.

"I MUST CALL 9-1-1."

With time the boys installed telephones in their apartments, making it easier for potential employers to contact them. And although this allowed for an onslaught of calls from their friends and relatives in Africa, volunteers recommended they install them in the event of an emergency. Should such an emergency arise, they were instructed to dial "9-1-1." There was one slight problem in these instructions, however, because the people who gave them failed to qualify the meaning of the word "emergency." As a result, the boys called the emergency hotline with any questions or concerns. If they needed directions to a job interview or to a friend's house, they called "9-1-1." If they injured themselves while playing soccer, they called "9-1-1." When needing assistance of any kind... they simply called "9-1-1."

One afternoon I received a frantic call from one of the boys. "Mom, I have a very bad problem!" he exclaimed. "What is it?" I asked. "The people here are trying to kill us." "What people?" "The people in charge of our house (the apartment manager). They are trying to poison us!" "Poison you?" *Here we go again...*"What on earth makes you think that?" I probed. "Well, while we were away, they came into our house without our permission. They opened all our cupboards and sprayed poison on our food. They knew that we would eat the food and that it would cause us to become dead. Even the small animals (roaches) are now dead. We had to throw everything away. All of our food is now gone and we have nothing left to eat." "Don't worry about the food," I assured him. "I'll bring you more food. But Jacob, you have to understand something, they were not trying to kill you. They only wanted to kill the small animals that live in your apartment. They sprayed inside your cabinets, because that is where the animals like to hide. They spray every apartment in your complex," I explained. "No, this is not right," he persisted. "Even my eyes and nose are burning from the poisons. They must be punished. I must call 9-1-1." I continued to plead with him to no avail, as he would not be persuaded. When hanging up the phone and ending our conversation, I knew without a shadow of a doubt that the next number he dialed would be "9-1-1."

"I NEED THE TEETH?"

The boys began to realize that many of their long-revered customs and rituals were not so readily accepted by the people in America. For instance, while living in Africa, they often held hands with one another in a non-sexual display of friendship and male camaraderie. However, when doing so in America, they were ridiculed and called homosexuals. Also to their dismay was the discovery that their most coveted rituals, such as scarification (scarring the skin to form designs) and the removal of some of the lower teeth, were also unacceptable to most Americans. After spending a lifetime considered as inferior, or abeeds (slaves), by the Arab Muslims of Northern Sudan, it was almost unbearable to think that the Americans might view them in the same light. Especially when they were now working full-time jobs and also attending school. The desire to "fit in," or to appear normal, proved particularly overwhelming for some of them who declined meals or refused medical attention in an effort to save money for dental implants. One boy, in need of serious medical attention, told me that he could not see a doctor because the doctor would ask him for money and he had to save his money for new teeth. "If I don't have the teeth, people will laugh at me. Even the girls will not speak to me without the teeth."

And while many of the boys have beautiful teeth due to a lack of sugar in their diets, others have considerable problems ranging from cavities and tooth loss to gross deformities. I took one of the boys to a local dentist to be fitted for dental implants, thinking that his lack of teeth on the bottom portion of his mouth was most likely due to tribal extractions or decay. However, after viewing the X-rays, the dentist informed me that the baby teeth were still impacted under the gums, most likely the result of severe malnutrition. I couldn't imagine how this young man had survived for so many years living in refugee camps with only grain and maize for his food and no lower teeth with which to eat it. Many of the dentists and orthodontists across the country have offered to assist the Lost Boys with their dental needs, but with the exception of a few, this has not been the case in Florida. In all fairness, this may be because many of the dentists in our state are not aware of this need. In that case, I hope this book will draw attention to the issue, not only in our state, but also in others.

"IT IS DECORATION!"

Also looked upon with curiosity and sometimes rebuke are the various decorations and markings on the faces and bodies of some of the boys. Some of them also have large holes in their earlobes, where they once sported ornaments such as bones, twigs, or decorative earrings while living in Africa. Most have discontinued wearing such ornaments since arriving in the U.S. for fear of rejection or that they might not be acceptable. However, others have found the desire to decorate their bodies to strong to abandon. Unable to find comparable earrings in America, or those acceptable by our society, some Lost Boys, like Johnson Kueth, have begun designing their own creations.

I got my first glimpse of Johnson's handiwork when stopping by his apartment to check on his sick housemate, Ezekiel. When I arrived Johnson was talking on the phone with one of his friends in Africa, and Ezekiel was nowhere to be found. I sat on the couch to wait, striking up a conversation in the meantime with a Muslim Somali refugee named Mohamed. (Although civil war has raged in Sudan between the Arab Muslims of the North and the Black Christian Animists of the South, some of the boys remain friendly with Muslims, understanding that not all of them share the same beliefs as those of their Sudanese government. But understandably there are those who still distrust all Muslims, grouping them together as one and regarding them with extreme caution.) As Mohamed and I sat talking, I happened to glance across the room at Johnson, noticing for the first time the bright pink earring protruding from his left ear. *Where on earth did he get that?* I wondered. Although I had seen various metal rods and other such ornaments in the ears of American youths, I had never seen a bright pink one such as this. Eventually my curiosity got the best of me, and I called out to him asking where he had found such an earring. "It is decoration," he answered with a proud smile across his face. *Well I can see that,* I thought. But I wanted to know where he had found it and what it was made of, so I walked across the room to get a better look. On closer examination, I immediately determined the origin of the earring and the revelation sent me into a fit of uncontrollable laughter. Intrigued by my reaction, Mohamed pleaded with me to tell him why I was laughing so much. "What is it?" he begged. "What has he put in his ear?" Of course I would have been more than happy to tell him, but I was laughing so hard that I couldn't even catch my breath.

As I already mentioned, Johnson's roommate was very sick and in constant pain, and his doctor had prescribed Darvocet in an effort to ease his discomfort. As you've probably guessed by now, Johnson had found one of the bright pink pills and decided that anything so beautiful must have surely been made to wear in his ears. And there you have it: African Jewelry Making 101!

Another episode involving "body decorations" took place at a local restaurant where I was enjoying lunch with two of the boys. I'm not sure why I hadn't noticed earlier, but all of a sudden my eyes were drawn toward Job's (not his real name) fingernails. But then again, why wouldn't they be, because they were painted bright red! *How do I explain this?* I thought. *I don't want to hurt his feelings, but at the same time I think we should discuss it.* "Who painted your fingernails?" I asked. "Oh, that girl," he replied. "You mean you paid someone to do it?" "No, that girl just did it. It is decoration," he said proudly. "We did it in Africa, in the camps. Some people even painted their teeth." *Oh my gosh!* I screamed inside my head. *They painted their teeth with fingernail polish?!* "Well, it's very beautiful," I mustered. "I'm sure that all the great warriors paint their fingernails and teeth. Some of the men in America paint their nails as well, like

125

musicians in rock bands. But you know, Job, when a man paints his nails bright red it can also send a signal that you might not want to send," I explained. "What signal is that?" he asked. "Well… for one thing it could signify that you enjoy the company of men instead of women." At this point, Joseph began to howl, falling out of his seat in a mock display of laughter. However, Job was still struggling to understand what I was talking about. Joseph began speaking in Arabic, a language that both boys understood, and suddenly Job's expression began to change from one of pride to that of sheer horror. Although it seemed difficult for him to speak at first, he was eventually able to utter a weak "Ohhhhh…" signifying that he finally understood. That was the last time I ever discussed the issue with Job. It was also the last time that he ever painted his fingernails bright red.

IS THIS REALLY REAL?

At the time of this writing, the Lost Boys have been living in the U.S. for more than three years. And while I'd like to say that our country is no longer such a mystery to them, it seems that they still sometimes struggle to distinguish between what is real and what is not, lending further credence to Sasha Chanoff's earlier concerns. For example, one night my family and I invited a group of Lost Boys to our house for dinner, as we often do. But on this particular night, we asked them to stay for a movie. My son and husband selected a *Star Wars* movie, knowing that the special effects and loud noises of the movie, when played on our big-screen television and surround-sound system, would surely astound them. The choice proved to be a good one, as evidenced in the loud laughter and constant chatter of the boys' native language. As usual, my attention was focused more on the reactions of the boys than the movie itself and in doing so, I couldn't help but feel a sense of pride for just how far these young men had come. In their initial days, they would most likely have been frightened or confused by a movie such as the one they were now watching. But instead they were laughing and talking, leading me to believe they had finally come to grips with the madness of American television and our society in general. My thoughts were soon interrupted by one of the boys tapping me on my shoulder. Pointing to the image of the alien Jar Jar Binks on the screen, he leaned over and quietly whispered in my ear "Mom, this is not really real, right?" he asked. "No sweetie, it's only make-believe," I assured him. To him, after seeing so many new and miraculous things in America, anything was possible, even the likes of Jar Jar Binks.

"YES, DOCTOR, I HAVE ONE VERY BAD PROBLEM."

The boys are often baffled by our medical system, finding our high-tech equipment and complicated jargon completely confusing—particularly in regard to the payment for services rendered. They cannot comprehend why anyone would expect them to pay for a doctor's visit, or subsequent tests, when no medicine or treatment is given for their illness. I don't think they really care what kind of treatment they receive, whether it's a prescription, aspirin, or M&Ms, they simply want something in their hands when they walk out the door other than just a bill.

Also confusing are the instructions given them when visiting doctors or labs, such as when a Lost Boy was sent to a lab for a series of tests, including a urine analysis. The lab technician asked him to collect a urine sample after giving him what she thought were adequate instructions on how to do so. Assuring her that he understood her instructions completely, he disappeared into the men's room, proudly placing the specimen jar inside the window as he exited. A short time later the technician returned asking to speak in private with the volunteer who had accompanied the boy. "We seem to have a slight problem," she told her. "Instead of urinating in the cup as requested, he seems to have spit into it."

Many trips to doctors with Lost Boys became adventures, out of which marvelous stories have been made. My personal favorite is that of Stephen Deng, who after receiving inconclusive findings on blood work was sent to an oncologist for further evaluation. Upon arriving at the oncologist's office, Stephen was assigned a physician's assistant to record his medical history, to be followed by a thorough exam. Like most people, she was extremely curious and fascinated by the tribal markings on his body, taking special note of the numerous scars that were most likely incurred while on the run across the wilds of Africa.

After completing the examination, the assistant asked Stephen if he had any additional problems or concerns he'd like to discuss with her. "Yes, Doctor, I have one very bad problem," he said. "What sort of problem is that?" she asked. In a mixed blend of British and Nuer he said, "I don't know what is happening to me. But my skeen is turning wheet." The assistant had no idea what he was trying to say, but I did, and because Stephen had recently teased me about my age, I decided to have a little fun with him. "Stephen, didn't they warn you before you left Kakuma that once you arrived in the U.S., your skin would turn white?" His eyes grew to the size of golf balls, as he looked first to the physician's assistant and then back at me, imploring one of us to tell him I was joking. But we both remained silent—a solemn look was our only response. Half laughing, half frightened to death, Stephen began to grow anxious. "No!

Really?" he pleaded. "Absolutely," I lied. "It happens all the time. I'm really shocked they didn't warn you about it in advance."

Stephen was just about ready for the crash cart at this point, and both the assistant and I were holding our sides in a vain effort to conceal our laughter. Not wishing to give him a heart attack, I finally confessed that I had been playing a joke on him. A flood of relief swept over his face, as the assistant explained that he was simply experiencing a condition called "ash" or dry skin. She reassured him further by telling him that it was only temporary and easily remedied with an over-the-counter body lotion. Feeling a little guilty for the mean trick that I had played on him, I bought him some of the lotion on the way home. When I called Stephen several days later to check up on him, he said, "I am really happy now. My skeen is now black again and I am myself!"

"I WILL HAVE TEN WIVES."

I guess one of the most difficult American customs the boys had to adjust to was that involving the number of wives allowed American men—or should I say the lack of wives allowed them! Not only was the concept of having "only" one wife completely foreign to them, but for most, it was absolutely unacceptable.

"I will go to Africa and I will bring back ten wives," declared one Lost Boy in a heated discussion on the issue. "Not if you plan on living in America," I countered. "And should you perhaps one day return to Africa and bring ten wives back to the U.S. with you, I suggest that you get to know them really well on the return flight. Because when you land in America, you're going to have to pick your favorite one and kiss the others goodbye." "I am a grown man now!" he roared. "Who will stop me? What can they do?" "I know you don't want to hear this," I continued, "but an American judge can stop you. It is the law of our land. And if you refuse to comply with his orders, he can even throw you in jail." "Then I will go to Canada!" he resolved. "Okay, if that's what you really want to do," I conceded. "But be sure to pack your warmest coat because the winters are really, really cold in Canada. In fact, there is sometimes so much snow on the ground that a person's body can disappear beneath it." He digested that last bit of information for just a moment, and then, in a final attempt to have the last word, snorted a defiant "Humph!" as he turned to walk away. And with that, the debate was over.

"THE ARABS HAVE FOUND US!"

"For many years, the people of Southern Sudan have been suffering and praying while the rest of the world lay sleeping. But on September 11, America was awakened…"

Bishop Nathaniel Garang, The Diocese of Bor

Some of the boys left wives behind in Africa, whom they had met and married while living in Kakuma. And although the thought of separating from them seemed unbearable, they knew it to be a necessary measure in order to ensure their survival, and in some cases, that of their children.

William Kou met his wife Abiei Jok Nhial at church services in Kakuma, and he says it was love at first sight. He courted her for almost a year before finally gathering the courage to ask her father for her hand in marriage. Much to his delight, her father agreed, but only under one condition: If William's name was selected among those for resettlement in the U.S., he must decline the offer and remain instead in Africa with Abiei. William says when faced with the decision of choosing between a new life in America and a life with the woman that he loved, the choice was an easy one. He chose Abiei.

Ten days later his name was posted on the board among those selected for resettlement in the U.S. "I had no regrets," says William. "I had already made my decision." When Abiei's father heard the news, he immediately sent for William, leading William to believe that he simply wanted to confirm his earlier agreement. But that was not Abiei's father's intentions at all, as he now knew William to be a man of his word. Abiei's father told William that he had played a trick on him when asking him to choose between a life in America and a life in Africa with his daughter. In doing so he had only been testing William in an effort to determine the depth of his love for Abiei. "Go to America," he instructed William, "but you must never forget my daughter."

A short time later William kissed Abiei goodbye, and then boarded a plane for America. He assumed that she would soon join him in the U.S., where together they would build a new life—a life filled with promise and hope for their future and that of their children. But this was not to be…

Soon after William arrived in America, the tragic events of September 11, 2001, took place, shaking the very core of our nation. Such an attack on American soil was previously unthinkable to us as Americans. But to the Lost Boys it was a familiar scene, one which they had experienced many times in their homeland. Fear ran rampant among many of the Lost Boys, who feared not only for themselves, but also for their American friends and mentors. "The

Arabs have come to punish the Americans," they cried, "because they have brought us here. No matter where we go or how hard we try to escape them, they always seem to find us."

Earlier in September, William's uncle, Jacob Bol Kon, along with 45 other Lost Boys, had departed Kakuma on a plane headed for America. With much anticipation, William planned to welcome Jacob to his new home in Jacksonville. As he watched the events of September 11 unfolding on television, and having no word from his uncle, William felt a sense of helplessness growing in the pit of his stomach. "Please, Dear God, don't let my uncle be on one of those planes," he prayed.

For the rest of the day and late into the night William waited anxiously by the phone for word from his uncle, but the phone remained silent. Each tap on the door brought with it a new spark of hope, but only disappointment greeted him. As one day rolled into the next, with still no word from his uncle, William finally resigned himself to the fact that Jacob had perished along with the countless others in the attacks on the World Trade Center. Added to his unbearable misery of being separated from his wife was the equally devastating realization that he had also lost his uncle and good friend, forever.

Eight days later, on September 19, William was greeted by a familiar voice on the telephone—that of his Uncle Jacob. Apparently he and the other passengers had been rerouted to Canada following the attacks. "It was really bad," Jacob told his nephew. "When the people aboard our plane heard about the attacks in America, they started screaming at us and calling us terrorists. They thought we were going to kill them because we looked different and spoke in another language. They truly believed that we were also terrorists!"

Although Lutheran Social Services had been alerted that Jacob and the others had been diverted to Canada, LSS had no idea that William was his relative and had been waiting for him. Therefore, they never relayed the message. "Why didn't you call me and tell me where you were?" pleaded William. "Because I didn't yet know how to use a telephone!" laughs Jacob.

Unfortunately, in an effort to protect our country from future attacks, our doors to freedom, long opened to refugees and immigrants from around the world, were tightly closed and no one knew when, or if, they would ever be opened again. Three long years later, following an endless paper trail and massive mounds of red tape, Abiei finally was able to join William in America. Together, they are building a new life beyond that of their wildest dreams. Joining them is their newborn son, Kou, the first child in either of their families for many generations to be born free.

"I HAVE BEEN BEING WITHOUT A MOMMY FOR SO LONG."

Even though the Lost Boys are now young men and prefer not to be called "boys" or "lost," the desire to reunite with their families, especially their mothers, has never diminished. And due in large part to the amazing technologies of the West such as the Internet, satellite communication, and telephones, that desire has become reality for many of them, who for the first time in seventeen years or longer have been able to speak with their lost relatives.

In doing so, they have unraveled many of the mysteries that have long surrounded their pasts, such as their true ages and also the fates of their friends and family. For the first time, they've heard eyewitness accounts from friends and relatives working with the various aid agencies in the South, who report that many of their mothers, fathers, brothers, and sisters, long presumed dead by the boys, are actually alive.

Of course, some of the boys have also received the devastating news that their entire families, or large portions of them, have been completely wiped out by enemy attacks, famine, or disease. Still, most say that bad news is better than no news at all, as it allows them closure and the ability to move on with their lives without the constant worry of the unknown. For those who are left in such limbo, like Jacob Angok, that uncertainty has hung over them like a dark cloud that never disappears.

I remember meeting Jacob for the first time as he finished playing soccer, wearing only his flip-flops for shoes. Several days after that, a young woman named Holli Seethaler called in response to a newspaper article written about the Lost Boys in our local paper and asked if she could somehow help. When I mentioned the possibility of volunteering or perhaps "adopting" one of the boys, she politely informed me that she had two small children of her own and simply didn't have the time. She asked if there was some other way she could help.

I proceeded to tell Holli about Jacob, mentioning that he had been playing soccer in flip-flops and asked if she might be able to buy him a pair of shoes. "Perfect!" she said. "I can do that." A few days later I gave the shoes to Jacob's roommate and asked him to pass them along. Later that night, Jacob called to thank me. "Mommieeee!" he said in a high-pitched voice that he uses when excited. "Thank you for my new shoes, they are really good. You know, Mom," he continued, "I have been being without a mommy for so long, I just want to thank you for being such a good mommy to me and for making me to be so happy." Jacob also shared with me his heartache in losing his own mother and father when he was only a child, saying that he had been despondent for months following the attack on their village that resulted in their separation. "I was in the darkness for a long time after that," he told me. "I was so sad, I didn't speak to anyone for at least three months."

The next day I called Holli to relay Jacob's thanks, sharing with her the heartbreaking story of how he had lost his own mother. She was so moved when hearing the story that she asked to meet him personally. The rest is history. Holli and Mike Seethaler, along with their two small children, Amanda and Michael, fell in love with Jacob Angok, unofficially "adopting" him into their own family. Not only is Jacob now employed in their family business, but he also joins them for family outings and holidays, as well as family vacations. Eventually Jacob was able to locate his birth mother, now living in a refugee camp in Nairobi. Unfortunately, Jacob learned that his father had passed away due to war-related circumstances.

"PEACE IN THE SUDAN?"

On January 6, 2002, rebel leaders from the SPLA-Nasir realigned themselves with the SPLA-Torit, becoming once again a united and formidable force in the South. But even more significant, on January 9, 2005, the SPLM/A and the Government of Sudan signed a Comprehensive Peace Agreement in Nairobi, Kenya, ending a civil war that has raged for over two decades.

Although I am extremely hopeful at the prospect of peace in the Sudan, my optimism and that of others who have followed this civil war is guarded at best. There is little doubt that the road ahead will be a long and hard one for the people of Southern Sudan as they begin rebuilding their war-torn country. As I and others anxiously await the outcome of their efforts, I can't help but wonder what significant roles the Lost Boys of America will play in the future of their country. In knowing them as I do, I'm sure that many of them will not only become key players in their government, but also respected members of their communities, including doctors, lawyers, and business professionals. It is my hope and belief that these incredibly courageous and intelligent young men will not only help to change the face of their nation, but also that of their people— a people who for generations have been viewed as insignificant not only by their own government, but also by those around the world who for so long have turned a blind eye to their suffering.

Lost Boy John Kuai told me that when fleeing his village in Southern Sudan, he had no idea what would become of his life. "As I ran through the bush, I paused, turning to catch one last glimpse of my beloved village, Juet. As I watched it burn before me in a mighty blaze, I saw a huge cloud of smoke rising in the sky, carrying everything I once knew and loved away from me, forever. At the time, I stood there like a statue, not knowing what to do next. I thought my life had truly ended. But God spoke to me on that day, telling me that He had a special purpose for my life. I knew that I must continue on my journey so that I could tell the rest of the world about the terrible things that had happened to my people and me. I must tell them that it was only God, and His Son Jesus Christ, who helped me to survive it."

Like John, I believe that each of these young men has a special purpose and calling in his life, a meaningful reason for having survived against all odds. And as peace returns once again to the Sudan, I look forward to the many possibilities that await them, as The Journey of the Lost Boys continues....

Jacob Angok at his job at the Seethalers printing company

Lynn Lamoureux, Joan Hecht, and Holli Seethaler

Stephen Wan at his accounting job in America

John Kuai, Simon Deng, and Ajak Atem Ajok

"Pappa Ray" & Maryellen Storms with Koul Anyang (left) and Abraham Kuany Chol (right)

John Kuai

136

William Kou and Abiei Jok Nhial – reunited at last

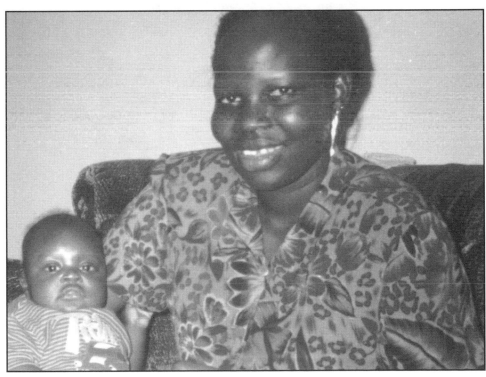

Abiei and baby Kou

137

Sharon Schade ©2005

Jacob Kon

Holli Sheethaler ©2005

In memory of John Dau

Johnson Kueth feeds the seagulls on a day at the beach

EPILOGUE

Sharon Schade ©2005

Ajak Atem Ajok*

Atem attends college with the hope of becoming a paralegal. Although his daily schedule is a grueling one, working full-time while also attending full-time classes, he continues to be committed to earning his college degree. Since arriving in America, Atem has been able to locate his mother, four sisters, and two half-brothers. He tells me that upon speaking to his mother for the first time, she hung the phone up on him, convinced that his mature voice could not be that of her son. "You are a grown man!" she cried. In her mind Atem was still a small child, even though many years had passed since she last saw him. Reluctantly, she later agreed to speak with him one more time, allowing him the opportunity to explain that he had now grown into a young man. In a final attempt to convince her of his true identity, Atem reminded her of the nickname that she had given him as a child, "Aporot," which is the name of a vegetable similar to okra. Atem says that she gave him this name because he was slippery like wet okra as a child, always wiggling around and hard to hold onto. In hearing the name, she became convinced that he was truly her son. Many tears followed that realization, both hers and Atem's.

Atem's mother tried her best to fill in the blank pages of his childhood, telling him many things about his family and also the events that had taken place since their separation—including the death of his father. Following the

140

attack on their village, his mother and father, along with their surviving children, had become displaced, left to wander aimlessly across the wilds of Africa without food, water, or shelter.

One day, while walking along a dirt road, GOS forces accosted them and commanded Atem's father to kneel before them on the ground. As his family stood helplessly by, they pointed a gun to his head, asking him if he was a Christian. His answer was "yes." They then commanded him to denounce his Christian faith or die. After he refused to do so, they executed him in full view of his wife and children. The soldiers then left his mother and his surviving siblings on the side of the road, most likely convinced that they would surely perish without food, water, or the protection of their husband and father. Miraculously they survived.

Atem has now become their sole supporter, providing school tuition for his four sisters and brother, as well as uniforms, food, and housing in a village located on the outskirts of Nairobi Town, Kenya. He regularly sends financial support to his mother as well, who lives in the Kakuma Refugee Camp. She greets his support with much reluctance, however, encouraging him instead to make his own "picture" (future) without concern for that of her own. I've often wished that she could see with her own eyes the beautiful picture that he has made, as it rivals any Van Gogh or Monet. It is the portrait of a champion, who is known among his people as "Kiir"– the River of Life. Atem has recently learned that his mother and siblings may soon join him in America, and he anxiously awaits their long-overdue reunion.

Joan Hecht ©2005

Abraham Kuany Chol

Abraham was the first Lost Boy in Jacksonville to complete his GED, earning his high school diploma within one year of his arrival. In addition to working full-time, he attends college full-time, hoping to one day become a surgeon. He is definitely off to a good start, earning a place on the Dean's list and the

President's Club at his junior college. And although he has little time for anything else except work and school, he hopes that all of his hard work and dedication will pay off so that he can one day return to Sudan and help his people. According to Dr. Pius Subek, Secretariat of Medicine for the SPLA, there are approximately ten doctors in all of Southern Sudan, currently attending to approximately eight million people.

Abraham Garang Ajak

While living in Kakuma, Abraham was reunited with many people from his past. Once again, he met the old man and his family who had taken him under their wings so many years ago. "This was a very good day," he says. "When the old man first greeted me, he said, 'God bless you. He is the one who took care of you all this time! You must always keep Him in your mind and use Him as your shield, for He will continue to protect you.'"

But most significant of all the reunions was that with his brother Peter, whom he had not seen or heard from in many years. True to his word, Peter brought news to Abraham regarding the fate of their parents. However, it was not the news that Abraham had hoped to receive. Peter told him that after leaving Pugnido, he had traveled to the distant country of Uganda where he found their sister Awei living with the family of their father's brother. She told him that she had remained with their parents for some time after fleeing their village in Sudan, but like many from the South, they had also become displaced. Eventually they joined with others forming a small caravan traveling throughout the African bush.

One day, after stopping to make camp for the night, Awei says that she left the camp's perimeter in search of fruit hanging from the trees. She told Peter that they were very weak by this time and in desperate need of food. Her parents, much too tired to join her, remained behind. Awei says that she had traveled for some time when she suddenly heard a thunderous sound from the direction of their camp. Fearing the worst, she ran back to see what had happened. "There was nothing left," she told him. "The government soldiers dropped bombs from the sky destroying our entire campsite. Everyone was killed, including our parents."

Peter remained in Uganda with Awei for another three years, never forgetting the promise that he had made to Abraham when he left him in Pugnido. Determined to find his brother, Peter eventually made his way to Kakuma. After learning of his parents' fate, Abraham says that there was only one thing left for him to do. He had to put his grief aside and move forward with his life, a life that eventually led him to the U.S.

Abraham never forgot his request from God when fleeing his village in Southern Sudan: "Dear God, please help to keep me alive so that I can be a future for my family." And after reaching America, he was finally able to fulfill his end of the bargain.

Abraham's brother, still living in Africa, contracted Kala-Azar disease soon after Abraham left. Kala-Azar is a parasitic disease spread by the bite of infected sand flies. Symptoms range from sores on the skin to swollen glands, fever, weight loss, enlarged spleen or liver, and abnormal blood test results. Left untreated, it weakens the immune system, often resulting in death. Due to a lack of treatment and poor living conditions in Southern Sudan, it has wiped out entire villages including the livestock. Even those who are fortunate enough to receive medical treatment often receive it too late and eventually die.

In order to provide the costly treatment that his brother needed, Abraham worked two jobs, consisting of twelve- to fourteen-hour workdays, seven days a week. He worked in extremely poor conditions that included exposure to insulation materials, which burned his eyes and caused sores on his body. His sacrifice and the hardships he endured ultimately proved to be his brother's salvation. However, Abraham downplays his role in caring for his brother saying, "I did what I must do, because I am the future of my family."

Joseph Gatkuoth Jiech

Joseph arrived in the U.S. on September 25, 2001. "I walked alone at that time," says Joseph. "No one came with me. I was given the number of the gate where I should board my plane, but when I attempted to do so, the man at security turned me away saying that I was boarding the wrong plane. I didn't realize that many planes left from one place and that mine had not yet arrived. It was very confusing. In hindsight," Joseph says, "I'm glad he stopped me. Otherwise I would have gone to Michigan instead of Florida and that would have been very bad."

Through the assistance of friends working with aid organizations in Southern Sudan, Joseph learned that his mother and sister were both alive and living in the Bentiu region. Sadly, he also learned that his father, along with his four brothers and three of his sisters had all passed away due to enemy attacks or famine-related illnesses and disease. When word reached his surviving sister that Joseph was in fact alive, she traveled to Khartoum by foot, a long and difficult journey, in order to speak with him by phone. The knowledge of his family's fate has been bittersweet, because it is difficult for him to accept the fact that he is the only remaining male in his family. Even more difficult is the burden of knowing that he cannot properly care for his mother and sister, because he has no way of contacting them or sending them money. "It is really hard," he says. "I have not seen or talked to my mother since I was a small boy, and now I am already a grown man."

Joseph works full-time when work is available, but has not yet enrolled in school due to his difficulties with the English language. However, he remains hopeful that he will one day be able to attend college and become a lawyer. He is attending English for Speakers of Other Languages (ESL) classes at a local college.

Sharon Schade ©2005

Johnson Mayiel Kueth

Johnson has located two of his brothers since he arrived in America, both of whom are now living in Khartoum City, Sudan. His middle brother Ngon, now 19 years old, lives with one of their father's brothers while his younger brother Pork, who is 17, lives with their father's sister.

Through the efforts of the International Committee of the Red Cross, Johnson was able to speak with both of his brothers by telephone for the first time in 12 years. They confirmed the deaths of their parents, but told him that their sister was seen alive and doing well, somewhere in the South of Sudan.

Johnson hopes to one day return to Sudan to visit his brothers and to search for his sister. When asked if he plans to live there, he says only, "I will have to think about that." In the meantime, he attends ESL classes in an effort to improve his English skills so that he can take his GED test and eventually enroll in college. He and his cousin Joseph Jiech are neighbors and continue to be the best of friends. While both express an interest in finding a wife and starting a family of their own, Johnson says that for now, "Life is good!"

Joan Hecht ©2005

Stephen Majak Deng

Stephen attended classes at a local high school for a brief time, but later dropped out due to his inability to support himself. "Without parents to support me," he says, "it is not possible for me to go to school." Stephen has also suffered from recurrent bouts of depression due to the uncertainty of his parents' fate. Like many from the South of Sudan, Stephen's parents seemed to have vanished from the face of the earth.

One afternoon, following a night shift, Stephen and his roommates were fast asleep when suddenly they were awakened by the loud ringing of the telephone. Normally, the obtrusive call would have gone unanswered, but for some reason, Stephen felt compelled to answer on that day. At the sound of his voice a woman began sobbing uncontrollably on the other end of the line, breaking only long enough to ask him, "Is this King II?" Stephen had not heard that name for a long time, and upon hearing it once again, a flood of memories swept over him. "King II" was the nickname that he had given to himself after seeing the word "king" in a textbook at his village school. "Kings have many cattle, like a rich man," says Stephen. He had reserved the name "King I" for his father. There was only one woman on earth who could know that name and Stephen realized that he was speaking to her at that very moment. For the first time in eleven years Stephen was speaking to his mother. "I have not heard your name mentioned in many years," she sobbed. "I thought that you were dead."

Stephen's roommates, hearing only his end of the conversation, soon put two and two together and began jumping and screaming in the background, making it difficult for him to hear what his mother was saying. "We have only five minutes," she warned him. Five minutes in which she must somehow reconstruct the childhood that was stolen from him so many years ago. "It was a very emotional time," he remembers. "But talking to my mom finally changed my sadness to happiness. There were no tears in my eyes, but my heart, it was really weeping." Although the call was brief, Stephen and his mother managed to reconstruct many of the missing parts of his life. Unfortunately, Stephen's father and sister had both died, but four brothers had survived and were now living with his mother in Bentiu. She told him that their life was very hard, due to a lack of rain that resulted in a shortage of food. Their only livestock, nine goats, were used as payment for speaking by phone with Stephen. Stephen suspects that someone who once knew him in Kakuma came to his mother's village when working with one of the aid organizations. That person had allowed her to use his satellite phone, although charging her an exorbitant fee to do so.

The loss of her livestock was a tremendous sacrifice, one that only a mother who truly loves her son would be willing to make. And it is with the knowledge of his mother's love that Stephen's life has changed completely. Once a young man consumed by sadness, Stephen now wants to be a "happy person" who makes people laugh (a comedian).

Sharon Schade ©2005

Peter Jal Kok

Many people have suggested that Peter seek a career in politics, as he makes friends easily, captivating them with his charming personality and infectious smile. However, they may also be shocked to know that underneath his confident exterior lie the torturous nightmares of a child long tormented by civil war and the loss of his family. Adding to the angst is the uncertainty of his true age. "I just want to know my age, Mama Joan. Can you imagine not even knowing how old you are?"

After searching for his family for many years to no avail, Peter received word that his brother had been spotted in the Gulu Refugee Camp in Northern Uganda. However, due to a lack of telephones or mail services in that area, it took several years for any of Peter's friends to locate him. "One day I answered the phone," says Peter, "and a voice on the other line said, "Male," (pronounced Mah-lay, meaning "hello" in the Nuer language) "I am your brother." It was the first time Peter had heard his brother's voice (also named Peter, with the middle name of Gatgon) in over 15 years. "At first I was skeptical of him," he says, "thinking that maybe he was trying to deceive me in order to obtain money from me. But then he told me many things about my family that only a close relative could know. Eventually I came to believe that he was truly my brother." In talking to his brother, Peter learned that his mother and father were also alive and living in the Bentiu region of Southern Sudan. And although Peter was unable to speak with them, his brother promised to send him photographs. "I am most curious to see if I look more like my mother or like my father. I also want to share my parents' photos with my American friends so that they can see what my family looks like." Peter learned that his five sisters were alive as well and also living with his parents in Bentiu.

But most importantly, Peter learned the answer to his lifelong question about his age. "You are 19 years old," his brother told him. In one brief phone call, Peter shed five years from his life, having assumed all this time that he was

24 years old. Later, Peter's brother-in-law also traveled by foot from Bentiu in order to speak with him by phone. This was a most wonderful thing for him to do, considering that he was not even a blood relative. "The distance he traveled," says Peter, "is equivalent to the distance from New York to Florida." For Peter, the joy of finding members of his family is immeasurable.

Peter attends classes at a local community college, planning to pursue a career in journalism. He also works full-time at a local health food store where, thankfully, his duties do not include cleaning the teeth of donkeys.

*On April 19, 2005, following seventeen years of separation due to civil war in Sudan, Ajak Atem Ajok was finally reunited with his mother and older brother Mabior (age 26). Joining them were his three younger sisters Ayak age 18, Abuk age 16, and Adau age 14, and his younger brother Ajok age 12 (the latter four of whom he has never met). Together they are working as a family to rebuild their lives in America, while also bringing hope to the many other Lost Boys and Lost Girls who pray for similar reunions with their own families.

"Now that I have found my mother and family," says Atem, "I think that I will be able to regain the childhood that I lost so many years ago." (Left front) Adau, Ajok, and Abuk. (Left rear) Mabior, Ayak, Achol, and Atem

Reunited at last, Atem and his mother Achol

Atem's younger sisters Abuk (front), Adau (center),
and Ayak (rear)

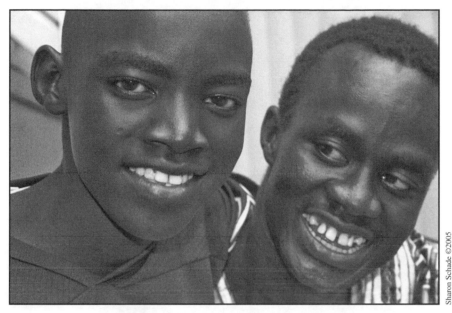

Atem and his younger brother Ajok

Atem welcomes his older brother Mabior to America

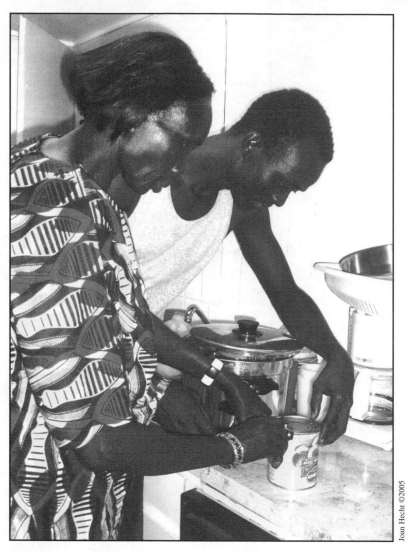

Atem instructing his mother on how to use a can opener, a role learned from his American mentors

This section is dedicated to the memories of Atem Ajok Deng (Atem's father), Amou Atem Ajak and Ayen Atem Ajok (his two younger sisters), and Deng Atem Ajak (his younger brother) all of whom perished as a result of the civil war in Sudan.

ACKNOWLEDGEMENTS

When first writing this book, I felt certain that I would finish it in several months' time. Several years later, I thought that it would never end. The experience has been one of the most emotional experiences of my life; one filled with laughter and tears, sorrow and joy, suffering, and most of all, "hope." It has been a journey that I shall never forget.

In the process, I have met many wonderful people who have in some way helped me to complete this project. Some have remained mere acquaintances, while others I now call friends. To each of you, I owe my deepest gratitude.

First and foremost I give my sincerest thanks to the Lost Boys featured in this book. I appreciate so much the time and effort you took in sharing your stories with me. I know that reliving your past was sometimes difficult. I only pray that your willingness to do so will in some way make a difference in the lives of those you left behind. A special thanks to those who worked behind the scenes as well such as John Kuai, Jacob Angok, William Wol Yol, Kuek Biar, John Dau, Peter Awai, Jacob Kon, William Kou, and Abiei Jok Nhial. The love, respect, and admiration that I feel for each of you is beyond words and without measure.

Adding immensely to the uniqueness and overall appearance of this book were the original drawings by Lost Boys John Yok, Isaac Tieng, Deng Deng Koch, and Awer Bul. Your talent speaks for itself, as do your giving spirits and generous hearts. Thank you!

Many others, both Sudanese and non-Sudanese, also shared of their time and knowledge to which I am forever grateful: Sasha Chanoff, David Chanoff, Roger Winter, Negussie Tesfa, John Prendergast, Martin Dawes, Diane and Denise Bennett, Opal Hardgrove, Helen Werking, "Mama Rachel" Obal, Dr. Pius Subek (Secretariat of Medicine and Commander of the SPLA) along with his beautiful wife Rose, Dr. David Chand, Ph.D, Stephen Wondu (Washington spokesperson for the SPLA), James Maluit Ruach (Director of the Sudan Relief and Rehabilitation Commission Inc.), Grace Ressler, Bishop Nathaniel Garang,

Christopher Jones, the Carpenters ABF class, Jacksonville Lost Boy volunteers, the staff of the Arizona Lost Boys Foundation, the staff of Freshministries, the staff of the Mayor of Jacksonville's Faith and Community-Based Partnerships, Sharon Schade, Paul Brim, Susan Winship, Deborah Martin, Laura Edwards and the staff at Raintree Graphics.

To my dear friends Holli and Mike Seethaler, Maryellen and Ray Storms, Lisa Brown and Lynn Lamoureux, your hearts are the genuine ones, and your friendship and support mean more to me than mere words could ever express. It is the humble hearts and giving spirits, such as yours, that make this world a better place to live. To Ruth and Sunny Rackley, Joe and Terri Largen, and Kathy Cope, thank you for your friendship and prayers. I felt them every step of the way. To my "older sisters" Rhona Ardizzoni and Beth Martin, my parents Bob and Mildred Honeycutt, and my in-laws Bill and Sonnie Hecht, thank you for your love and support. To my editor Laurie White, I can't believe we finally did it! It has been my utmost pleasure to work with you. To my pseudo editors Bill Hecht, Mildred Honeycutt, and Brian Polding, thank you! To my best friends since childhood Gail Ingalls, Rhonda Edwards, Rosilyn Robertson, and Leslie Smith, thanks for being there.

An extra special thanks to Joung-ah Ghedini, Ellen Bole, Lilli Tnaib, and Anne Kellner of the UNHCR for taking the time and energy to help me obtain many of the incredible photographs in this book. Your contributions and those of the UNHCR have been invaluable and greatly appreciated. To Wendy Stone, whose famous photographs have been used in many documentary films and publications around the world, thank you for allowing us to see through your eyes the suffering of the Sudanese people, in particular the Lost Boys and Lost Girls. Thanks to each of you for helping to make this book a better one.

I am also extremely thankful to God for the mighty way that He has worked in my life, including His allowing me the opportunity of meeting the Lost Boys and to write their incredible story. I am so humbled to be used by Him and give Him all the glory.

To my family and friends who have so patiently allowed me to pursue this calling, thank you for your love and support. I hope that in reading this book my husband and children will one day understand why I spent so many hours tapping away on the computer. I love you more than the moon and stars and all the Godiva chocolate in the world!

Finally, I've chosen to end this book in the same manner that I began it: by stepping outside the box. In its current format, I was forced to omit the one story (about Ezekiel Kong Deng) that originally inspired me to write it. Somehow, when all was said and done, it just didn't seem to fit in the main text of the book. Perhaps it just needs special recognition of its own.

Ezekiel Kong Deng

I had the pleasure of meeting Ezekiel shortly after his arrival to America and from the very beginning, he claimed a special place in my heart. You see, when my son Evan was born, in accordance with my husband's Jewish faith, we were required to give him two sets of names. His English name which is Evan, and also a special Hebrew name that would somehow make a statement about the type of person we hoped our son would become. It was to be a name that linked us to a special loved one who had passed away, a name that would help us to remember them in a special light. The name we chose was Ezekiel, which means the "The strength of God." I later joked with Ezekiel about the fact that God had given me two sons with the very same name. Little did I know at the time what a special remembrance that name would bring.

Ezekiel was extremely frail when he first arrived in Jacksonville. Even the simplest of tasks such as walking next door to visit his "brothers" was sometimes difficult. We later learned that he had contracted the hepatitis B virus while living in Africa, which left untreated for years had caused irreversible damage to his liver. After many visits to the doctor and later liver specialists, it was determined that his liver was in fact failing and that a transplant was needed in order for him to survive. Miraculously, Mayo Clinic offered to perform the transplant and a flurry of tests, x-rays, and minor surgical procedures followed.

Many people didn't realize just how sick Ezekiel was, in part, because he never complained. Even when suffering the most and understanding that he may be dying, he always smiled and claimed to be "feeling in good health!" But at one point, he confided in me saying, "Mama Joan, maybe God in all His glory brought me to this place, America, so that I should see this before I die." I tried to encourage him by telling him that I thought God's plans for him were much bigger than that and I truly believed it.

At his request, I accompanied him to many of his frequent doctor appointments, and in the process of spending so much time together, we became

155

extremely close. Ezekiel began to share many of his innermost thoughts with me, which was a huge step considering the fact that I'm a woman. Even though he thought of me as his mother, it is not the custom of men in his country to discuss anything of importance with women. In fact, he once told me that if he were still in Africa, he would not discuss personal issues such as his medical history with women at all. And if a woman were to ask him such questions, he would tell her to go and talk with the other women or to go cook him something to eat. I informed him that he was now living in America and if he told a woman to go cook him something to eat, she would most likely tell him to go cook it himself! He laughed, understanding that things are much different in America, resigning himself to the fact that his ways of thinking might have to change.

On June 23, 2002, at approximately 11:15 p.m., roughly four weeks after Ezekiel was placed on the transplant list, I received a phone call from one of the Lost Boys. He informed me that he was calling on Ezekiel's behalf, which immediately caused me to worry as Ezekiel generally called me himself. He quickly assured me that Ezekiel was fine, and that he was calling only because Ezekiel had a doctor's appointment at 5 a.m. the next morning and could I take him. I was still unused to the manner in which the boys frequently called at the last minute when needing a favor, and therefore I responded in a louder tone than usual. "HE HAS A DOCTOR'S APPOINTMENT AT 5 A.M. TOMORROW MORNING AND YOU'RE CALLING ME AT 11:00 P.M. THE NIGHT BEFORE TO TELL ME ABOUT IT?! I shouted. "How long has he known about this?" "They just called him," he said. "They called him this late at night?" I asked. *That didn't sound right...* Then, suddenly it hit me like a ton of bricks and my heart began to race. "Are you trying to tell me that they're going to do the liver transplant tomorrow?" His reply: "The liver is waiting."

In the midst of all the excitement, I couldn't help but pause and think of the person who had died in order to provide this liver for Ezekiel. They told us that it was a young liver and I knew that somewhere a mother had lost her child so that Ezekiel could live. After hugs, prayers, and tearful best wishes, Ezekiel entered the operating room with a smile on his face and hope in his heart.

The surgery was a lengthy one, filled with unexpected complications and the night that followed was no better. Ezekiel experienced significant blood loss during the surgery and through the night, requiring additional surgery the next morning. Following the surgery, while sitting in the waiting room, I had the strangest sensation that Ezekiel needed me so I went to him. As I stood beside his bed, he began to move his hand erratically, as if trying to remove the bed sheet. (His hands were restrained to prevent him from ripping out the IV and breathing tube.) It occurred to me that he might simply want to hold my hand, so I asked him and he nodded yes. By this time, his body began to jerk involuntarily and I tried desperately to calm him. Not quite knowing what to do, I asked if he wanted me to sing to him. Once again he nodded his head. I sang all three verses of Amazing Grace, a song that I have sung since childhood, but at that particular time it was the most difficult song I've ever had to sing. And although his eyes were swollen shut, I couldn't help but notice a tear as it rolled down his cheek. I only pray that my presence in some way comforted him.

One of his doctors called me from the room, informing me that Ezekiel's condition was grave and that he would require another liver transplant. He told me that Ezekiel had been placed as top priority on the national donor list.

He was given medication to help alleviate his pain and I returned to the waiting room allowing him the opportunity to rest. A short time later, a nurse came for me. With tears in her eyes she explained that Ezekiel had taken a turn for the worse and that as his designated guardian and caregiver, the doctors wished to speak with me in the "quiet room." I knew in my heart I would not receive the news that I so desperately wanted to hear.

After waiting for twenty minutes with no word from the doctors, I decided to see for myself what was going on. As I approached the hallway to Ezekiel's room, I noticed doctors and nurses running in every direction carrying all types of equipment, some with tears in their eyes. The doctor who had performed the transplant approached me, telling me how saddened he was by this turn of events. "We didn't expect this to happen," he said. "We had hoped for a much different outcome." We all had, but it appeared that it was not to be. I made only one request, one that the doctor so graciously granted. "Ezekiel has been alone his whole life," I explained. "I don't want him to be alone when he dies. If all attempts to save him fail, please let me be with him for his final moments." And then, as I waited in the hospital hallway, tears falling from my eyes, an all-consuming peace suddenly filled me. I wish I could explain it, but it was "a peace that passes all understanding." I knew that Ezekiel would soon be going home.

A short time later I stood by Ezekiel's side, his hand in mine, and told him that God was waiting for him, His arms opened wide, calling him by name into His kingdom where He had prepared a beautiful mansion for him. I also told Ezekiel how much knowing him had meant to me and how very much I loved him. I told him that my life was so much better for having known him. "It's okay to let go," I told him. "I'll see you again one day." All efforts to resuscitate him were stopped a short time later and Ezekiel Kong Deng was pronounced dead. His journey here on earth was over.

I realize that to many of you hearing this story for the first time it may in fact seem as if "God in all His glory" brought Ezekiel to America "just to see this wonderful place" before he died. But we can never underestimate God's intentions. I still believe them to be much bigger than that. I think God brought Ezekiel to this country in a time when there is so much hatred and terror to be a living example to us all.

Ezekiel Kong Deng touched people from all walks of life: Christians, Jews, Buddhists, Muslims, black, white, rich, and poor. We were like a large pot of stew filled with many different ingredients and Ezekiel was the spoon that stirred our souls. He stirred in us the ability to step out of our boxes, to reach beyond our comfort zones and care for our fellow man regardless of our differences or the color of our skin. I will hold him in my thoughts and heart forever and I will love and miss him always.

NOTES

The majority of the text recorded within this book was gathered in personal interviews between various Lost Boys or other Sudanese individuals and me. However, I have taken every measure possible to verify that information, as listed in the numerous publications below. I have also gathered additional information from many of those sources, which has been noted as such. Any direct quotes have been noted by quotation marks.

In an effort to ensure easier readability, I have also taken the liberty of correcting grammatical and linguistic errors when necessary. *Please note that the historical information recorded in this book does not necessarily reflect the views of the Lost Boys or other individuals interviewed by the author.

A GLIMPSE OF AFRICA

In addition to my personal experiences and the interviews with the Lost Boys, I also obtained information through interviews with Helen Werking, Rachel Obal, and Venda Buchac of Lutheran Social Services in Jacksonville, FL.

Pg. 5 ...approximately thirty-eight hundred of the young refugees... See *Sudanese (Kakuma) Youth,*
http://www.state.gov/g/prm/rls/fs/2001/3398.htm accessed 2/3/2003

SUDAN: THE BEGINNING

Pg. 16 There are reportedly 600... http://www.abc-usa.org/resources/resol/Sudan.htm accessed 3/13/2005

Pg. 16 When all was said and done, the British named... Jok, *War and Slavery in Sudan,* pg. 17

Pg. 17 Initially, Nimeiri received support from the Soviet Union…,…. See Scroggins, *Emma's War*, pgs. 37-38

Pg. 17 According to the terms of the Addis Ababa Treaty…,… Ibid. pgs. 37-38

Pg. 18 …with weapons supplied by Libya, formed a new version…, See J. Millard Burr and Robert O. Collins, *Requiem for the Sudan*, Pg. 13-14

Pg. 18 In the midst of rebel uprisings in the South… See Scroggins, *Emma's War*, pg. 38

Pg. 18 John Garang was not ….. See J. Millard Burr and Robert O. Collins, *Requiem for the Sudan*, pg. 12

Pg. 18 Garang had been privy to the inner workings of the Nimeiri…, … with the mutinous soldiers of the 105th battalion. Ibid. pgs. 12-13

Pg. 19 Together, the rebel soldiers fled to neighboring Ethiopia where they were welcomed…See Scroggins, *Emma's War,* pg.185

Pg. 19 …"establish the united socialist Sudan, not a separate Sudan." Ibid. pg. 13

Pg. 19 …but a small faction joined GOS forces,… See Human Rights Watch Africa, *Civilian Devastation* pg. 20-21

Pg. 19 In 1983, soon after the defection…See J. Millard Burr and Robert O. Collins, *Requiem for the Sudan,* pg. 15

Pg. 19 …Garang was a Dinka, all Dinkas were SPLM/A supporters… Ibid. pg. 19

Pg. 19 …enlisting the help of area tribes such as the Baqqara (later known as the Murahileen…, …to kill their own people See Jok Madut Jok, *War and Slavery in Sudan* pgs. 6, 12, 28-29, 100, 119- 120

Pg. 20 Those who survived this crusade… Ibid. pg. 100

Pg. 20 Some of these women and children (boys and girls alike)… Ibid. pgs. 33-41

Pg. 20 The young boys and men still remaining…, See Human Rights Watch Africa, *Civilian Devastation* pg. 3

Pg. 20 …one that Garang has reportedly denied… See Human Rights Watch Africa, *Civilian Devastation,* pg. 197, J. Millard Burr and Robert O. Collins*, Requiem for the Sudan*, pg. 300

Pg. 21 ...an estimated 20,000 Sudanese children have become separated... See Church World Services *"The story of the Lost Boys"* www.churchworldservice.org/immigration/sudan/background.htm accessed 1/25/2003

AJAK ATEM AJOK

Unless otherwise noted, all content in this segment was obtained through personal interviews between the author and Atem.

Pg. 22 The Dinka tribe, the single largest ethnic group in Sudan,... See Human Rights Watch Africa, *Civilian Devastation* Pg. 10

Pg. 26 ...shouting "Lour, Lour!" Translation provided to the author by Deborah Martin

ABRAHAM KUANY CHOL

Unless otherwise noted, content in this segment was obtained through personal interviews between the author, Abraham Chol, and Rachel Obal. (Because Abraham was so young at the time he fled his village, it was sometimes difficult for him to remember, with much detail, the everyday lifestyle of his people. Therefore, Rachel Obal stepped in to fill in some of the interesting facts of their daily life. Although Rachel is originally from the Anuak region, she is very knowledgeable about the Sudanese culture as a whole.

Pg. 36 The total number of captives at any given time is estimated at 10,000 to 15,000." See Jok Madut Jok, *War and Slavery in Sudan* pg. 1

ETHIOPIA: A PLACE OF REFUGE

Unless otherwise noted, information reported in this segment was gathered through correspondence between the author, Negussie Tesfa, Roger Winter, and Dr Pius Subeck, (Secretariat of Medicine and Commander in the SPLA), and through numerous interviews with various Lost Boys, such as Peter Kok, Atem Ajak, Peter Bol, Stephen Deng, and others who wish to remain unknown.

Pg. 40 Roger Winter, former... As relayed to the author by Roger Winter in telephone interview.

Pg. 40 For the most part, the boys were placed... See Human Rights Watch Africa, *Civilian Devastation*, pg. 206

Pg. 41 They had instead been willingly handed over to the SPLA... See Scroggins, *Emma's War*, pg. 140

Pg. 42 Many of the Lost Boys from the Nuer region... See Human Rights Watch Africa, *Civilian Devastation*, pg. 206

Pg. 42 Pugnido hosted the largest number of unaccompanied minors..., Ibid pg. 206

Pg. 42 It is close in proximity to the small town of Panyido... As reported through email correspondence with aide worker Marie Lusted on 2/5/2003

Pg. 42 One of the boys told me...As relayed to the author by Peter Bol.

Pg. 42 The climate is very hot in Pugnido, similar...See *3 History of the War Refugees* http://www.cbu.dataphone.se/flyktingbarnteamet/3olle.htm accessed 2/5/2003

Pg. 42 ...the boys were divided into different groups of about 30 boys per tukul., ... Ibid. accessed 2/5/2003

Pg. 43 A portion of the Gilo River flowed... obtained by the authors in interviews with various Lost Boys and also Negussie Tesfa.

Pgs. 45-46 In 1985, while visiting the United States ..., ...See J. Millard Burr and Robert O. Collins, *Requiem for Sudan,* pgs. 2-3, Sudan: The Transitional Military Council http://lcweb2.loc.gov/cgibin/query/r?frd/cstdy:@field(DOCID+sd0041) Accessed 7/18/03, *Sudan: A Historical Perspective* http://www.sudan.net/government/history.html Accessed 3/18/2003, *Sudan Home* http://sudanhome.com/info/sadiq.htm Accessed 2/28/03, Human Rights watch, *Civilian Devastation*, pgs. 8-9

Pg. 46 It was for these reasons, along with the prospect of a successful peace agreement with Southern Rebels,...as reported to the author by Roger Winter.

ABRAHAM GARANG AJAK

All information in this section was obtained through personal interviews between the author and Abraham Garang Ajak.

JOHNSON MAYIEL KUETH

All information recorded in this section was obtained through personal interviews between the author, Johnson Mayiel Kueth, and Joseph Jiech.

ESCAPE FROM ETHIOPIA

Unless otherwise noted, all information recorded in this section was gathered by the author through personal interviews with Lost Boys, Negussie Tesfa, and Bishop Nathaniel Garang.

Pg. 58 Some of those suffering the greatest impact... See Human Rights Watch/ Africa. *Civilian Devastation,* pg. 23

Pg. 58 Mengistu had long battled with..., ... See Flying Fish- *Eritrea, Ethiopia, War & Famine; Hale Selassie, Mengistu & IMF,* http://www.flyingfish.org.uk/articles/eritrea/strawbs.htm accessed on 8/15/03

Pgs. 58-60 The Sudanese refugees, particularly the Lost Boys...,...Information obtained by the author through interviews with various Lost Boys (some whom wish to remain anonymous) and Negussie Tesfa.

THE GILO RIVER

Information recorded in this section was obtained through personal interviews between the author, various Lost Boys, Negussie Tesfa, and Bishop Nathaniel Garang.

JOSEPH GATKUOTH JIECH

Unless otherwise noted, information recorded in this section was obtained through personal interviews between the author, Joseph Jiech, and Johnson Kueth.

Pg. 66 But in reality, they are considered to be some of the most dangerous animals... Hippos are particularly aggressive when disturbed,... *River Hippopotamus,* http://www.ultimateungulate.com/riverhippo.html Accessed 2/22/03

Pg. 70 Sometimes these lines are cut so deep... See *"The Dinka of the Southern Sudan,"* http://www.hsc.csu.edu.au/pta/scansw/dinka.htm accessed 2/17/03

SUDAN: THE NIGHTMARE RETURNS

Unless otherwise noted, information recorded in this section was obtained through personal interviews with various Lost Boys including Jacob Kon, Abraham Kuany, Simon Deng, John Dau (and others who wish to remain unknown), along with Wendy Stone.

Pg. 74 ...in numbers of nearly 16,000...this number was given to the author by various Lost Boys interviewed.

Pg. 74 ... journeyed to Pochala (Pa-cho-la),... See Human Rights Watch/ Africa. Civilian Devastation, pgs. 23-24

Pg. 74 ...while the majority of those fleeing from Itang traveled to Nasir with the exception of a small portion that headed for Pochala. See Scroggins, *Emma's War,* pg. 215

Pg. 74 in Pochala were assisted primarily by the SPLA and the International Committee of the Red Cross (ICRC). See Human Rights Watch/Africa. *Civilian Devastation*, pgs. 209, 211-212,

Pg. 75 According to various surveys...Ibid. pgs. 211-212

Pgs. 75-76 The story of Mrs. Stone in Nasir was relayed to the author in a telephone interview with Mrs. Stone.

Pg. 76 In August of 1991,...See J. Millard Burr and Robert O. Collins, *Requiem for Sudan*, pgs. 299-300

Pg. 76 This charge later boomeranged, however,... See *Sudan,* http://www.hrw.org/reports/1995/Sudan.htm accessed 3/27/2003

Pg. 76 SPLA spokesperson...taken from a telephone interview between the author and Mr. Wondu.

Pg. 76 ...giving credence to the propaganda that the civil war of Sudan was a battle among tribes... See Jok Madut Jok, *War and Slavery in Sudan,* pgs. 127-128

Pg. 77 ...the GOS reportedly... See Scroggins, *Emma's War,* pgs. 287,294

Pg. 77 ...launching a full-scale attack against Garang's hometown district of Bor. For more detailed accounts of this conflict, See Scroggins, *Emma's War* and Human Rights Watch/Africa. *Civilian Devastation.*

Pg. 77 Meanwhile, Ethiopian rebels, aligned with the GOS... See Scroggins, *Emma's War*, pg. 193

Pg. 77 …directing guided missiles toward their camps in Pochala from nearby Ethiopian borders. See Human Rights Watch/ Africa, *Civilian Devastation* pg. 212

Pg. 77 …the children dug foxholes outside…As reported by Lost Boys interviewed by the author.

Pg. 78 As land and air assaults against… See Human Rights Watch/Africa, *Civilian Devastation,* pg. 38

Pg. 78 …in search of the Amoyoak roots… As relayed to the author by Lost Boy John Kuai.

Pg. 79 …where much to their surprise they were greeted by a lone ICRC aid worker. As reported to the author by the late John Dau. (I made numerous attempts to find this woman through the local and International Red Cross to no avail. I really have very little information about her except that her first name is Ayako and that she is possibly British. I wish I could have heard in her own words the magnitude of what she witnessed that day. But most of all, I wish I could have told her that her heroic efforts were not in vain. I'm sure that there are many other unsung heroes in this tragic story. People, like Ayako, who laid their lives on the line to help these young boys and others like them. Whoever or wherever you are, I speak on behalf of all those who love these young men when I say thank you and may God bless you abundantly for your selfless deeds.

Pg. 80 Adding to their treacherous walk were encounters with unfriendly tribesmen of the time, such as the fierce Toposa warriors…Taken from interviews with numerous Lost Boys including Jacob Angok, Peter Kok, John Kuai, Daniel Deng and John Dau. Similar accountings are cited in Human Rights Watch/Africa, *Civilian Devastation,* pgs. 38, 212

Pg. 80 And under a barrage of heavy gunfire… as reported to the author in interviews with various Lost Boys and also in Human Rights Watch/Africa, *Civilian Devastation,* pg. 48

STEPHEN MAJAK DENG

Unless otherwise noted, information recorded in this segment was obtained through personal interviews between the author and Stephen Deng.

Pg. 85 It is reported that 3-5 displaced children in Southern Sudan…As reported by Dennis E. Bennett, founder of Servant's Heart

KAKUMA REFUGEE CAMP

Unless otherwise noted, information in this segment was obtained through personal interviews between the author and various Lost Boys, as well as Sasha Chanoff and Bishop Nathaniel Garang.

Pg. 89 Kakuma, located in the northwestern tip....

The conditions of Kakuma, as reported in this segment, were taken from personal interviews between the author, various Lost Boys and Sasha Chanoff as well as in a published report on the internet by Relief Web, *ACT Appeal Kenya: Kakuma Refugee Camp* –AFKE-32.
http://www.reliefweb.int/w/rwb.nsf/9ca65951ee22658ec125663300408599/9e e257a3f481bf29... accessed 2/3/2003

Pg. 90 ...the camp's population now surpasses 80,000,... See Refugees International- *Kakuma: A Troubled Refugee Camp in Kenya*, http://www.refintl.org/content/article/detail/910/&output=printer?PHPS ESSID=f798e7a88ebb2c12b56fe0df2cf5390a

PETER JAL KOK

Unless otherwise noted, contents of this story were obtained through personal interviews between the author and Peter Kok.

Pg. 96 However, the promises made by the Kenyan government... As reported to the author by William Kou.

Pg. 98 Using plastic jugs left over from their water rations,... As reported to the author by the late John Dau and Bishop Nathaniel Garang.

Pg. 101 Others, like Peter's housemate B'bol... As reported to the author by B'bol (also known as John Biel) and Peter Kok.

WELCOME TO AMERICA

In addition to my personal experiences with the Lost Boys, I collected additional information through personal interviews with Helen Werking, Rachel Obal, Venda Buchac (Lutheran Social Services of Jacksonville, FL), Maryellen and Ray Storms, and Holli Seethaler.

Pg. 122 Both the volunteers and management were perplexed by their actions and... Taken from a conversation between the author and Lost Boy Simon Arop.

BIBLIOGRAPHY

Burr Millard J., and Robert O. Collins, *Requiem for the Sudan: War, Drought, and Disaster Relief on the Nile.* Boulder, Co: Westview Press, 1995.

Human Rights Watch / Africa. *Civilian Devastation: Abuses by All Parties in the War in Southern Sudan.* New York: Human Rights Watch, June 1994.

Human Rights Watch/Africa. *CHILDREN IN SUDAN: Slaves, Street Children and Child Soldiers* Human Rights Watch, September 1995.

Jok, Madut Jok. *War and Slavery in Sudan.* University of Pennsylvania Press, 2001.

Scroggins, Deborah. Emma's War: An Aide Worker, a Warlord, Radical Islam, and the Politics of Oil: A True Story of Love and Death in Sudan. New York: Panthcon, 2002.

Internet Listings

http://www.state.gov/g/prm/rls/fs/2001/3398.htm *Sudanese (Kakuma) Youth*
http://www.abc-usa.org/resources/resol/Sudan.htm

Church World Services "The story of the Lost Boys" www.churchworldservice.org/immigration/sudan/background.htm Church World Services *"The Story of the Lost Boys"*

htp://www.cbu.dataphone.se/flyktingbarnteamet/3olle.htm ***Olle Jeppsson.** 3 History of the War Refugees.*

January, 1994

http://www.sudan.net/government/history.html *Sudan: A Historical Perspective* http://sudanhome.com/info/sadiq.htm Sudan Home. *SADIQ AL MAHDI & COALITION GOVERNMENTS*

http://www.flyingfish.org.uk/articles/eritrea/strawbs.htm *Flying Fish-Eritrea, Ethiopia, war & famine; Hale Selassie, Mengistu & IMF*

http://www.ultimateungulate.com/riverhippo.html *River Hippopototamus*

http://www.hsc.csu.edu.au/pta/scansw/dinka.htm *"The Dinka of the Southern Sudan"*

http://www.hrw.org/reports/1995/Sudan.htm *Sudan*

http://www.refintl.org/content/article/detail/910/&output=printer?PHPSES-SID=f798e7a88ebb2c12b56fe0df2cf5390a Refugees International. *Kakuma: A Troubled Refugee Camp in Kenya*

http://www.reliefweb.int/w/rwb.nsf/9ca65951ee22658ec125663300408599/9e e257a3f481bf29... Relief Web: ACT Appeal Kenya: Kakuma Refugee Camp –AFKE-32